COUNTERTERRORISM: FEDERAL RESEARCH AND DEVELOPMENT, ORGANIZATION, POLICY AND FUNDING

COUNTERTERRORISM: FEDERAL RESEARCH AND DEVELOPMENT, ORGANIZATION, POLICY AND FUNDING

GENEVIEVE J. KNEZO

Novinka Books
New York

Library of Congress Cataloging-in-Publication Data
Available Upon Request

ISBN: 1-59033-637-2.

Nova Science Publishers, Inc.
400 Oser Ave, Suite 1600
Hauppauge, New York 11788-3619
Tele. 631-231-7269 Fax 631-231-8175
e-mail: Novascience@earthlink.net
Web Site: http://www.novapublishers.com

Printed in the United States of America

CONTENTS

PREFACE

Before the September 11th terrorist attacks, experts questioned whether the government was prepared adequately to conduct and use research and development (R&D) to counter terrorism. They cited inadequate planning; conflicting information about agency funding; the absence of coordinated ways to set priorities and eliminate duplication; and the need to use research resources effectively. Mechanisms have been established since then to set specific R&D priorities and to coordinate interagency policy. The Office of Homeland Security (OHS), created by Executive Order 13228, does not list R&D among its major responsibilities, but R&D is a topic of one of the interagency Policy Coordination Committees attached to the Homeland Security Council (HSC), OHS's interagency group. The director of the Office of Science and Technology Policy (OSTP) was not named to participate in OHS activities, but an OSTP staff member is filling the HSC interagency R&D policy coordination role. The President gave OSTP responsibilities for policies regarding foreign student visas, foreign enrollment in "sensitive" courses, and technology for immigration. The National Science and Technology Council, an interagency body, staffed by OSTP, has five antiterrorism R&D working groups.

Proposals have been made to expand the interagency Technical Support Working Group and the Defense Department's Defense Advanced Research Projects Agency, which have funded counterterrorism R&D in the past. The House passed H.R. 5005, an amended version of legislation that the President sent to Congress to create a Department of Homeland Security (DHS) which would plan, fund, and coordinate some R&D. S. 2452, the Lieberman substitute agreed to by the Governmental Affairs Committee, would give broader R&D authority to a national homeland security department. Each proposal would create different kinds of units to analyze and evaluate counterterrorism technologies before procurement and deployment and to coordinate some federal counterterrorism R&D. The President's FY2003 counterterrorism R&D budget request was $3 billion; the DHS envisioned in H.R. 5005 would handle about 17% of this, comprised of about $300 million of newly authorized R&D and between $200 to $300 million of already authorized R&D to be transferred to the proposed department.

Bioterrorism R&D funding is managed largely by the Defense and Health and Human Services departments. Each agency has intra-agency coordination mechanisms, and formal interagency groups have been established. The interagency President's Critical Infrastructure Board has responsibility for information security R&D; OSTP was tasked to help it coordinate R&D priorities and the board was authorized to request federal agencies to fund priority R&D programs.

Among the issues to be considered in creating a new homeland security department with R&D responsibilities are: which R&D areas should be transferred; can other related R&D be coordinated effectively and without erecting barriers between the conduct of civilian and security-related R&D; and how should the existing counterterrorism R&D coordination mechanisms in OSTP, OHS and other departments be linked to a homeland security department with R&D responsibilities?

Chapter 1

INTRODUCTION

Since the September 11th terrorist attacks, federal activities and organization for Counterterrorism research and development (R&D) have evolved. This report inventories federal agency Counterterrorism R&D funding patterns, programs, and priority-setting and coordination mechanisms, and assesses changes proposed. The report describes developments in federal organization to set priorities and coordinate R&D in the Office of Science and Technology Policy (OSTP), the Office of Homeland Security (OHS), and related bodies. It also describes how R&D would be managed and coordinated in the major legislative proposals to create a homeland security department, and assesses these arrangements. Issues arising from legislative proposals to centralize R&D in a homeland security department include: identifying which R&D areas should be transferred to a department; deciding whether other related R&D can be coordinated effectively and without erecting barriers between the conduct of civilian and security-related R&D; and determining if and how the existing counterterrorism R&D coordination mechanisms in OSTP, OHS and other departments should be linked to a homeland security department with R&D responsibilities. The topics of bioterrorism R&D and information security R&D are covered as case studies in the appendix because they received considerable attention both before and after the September 11 attacks and they illustrate different kinds of coordination mechanisms that have been established.

A list of acronyms used in this chapter appears in the appendix.

Chapter 2

FEDERAL AGENCY FUNDING AND PROGRAMS FOR COUNTERTERRORISM R&D

The Office of Management and Budget's *Annual Report to Congress on Combating Terrorism, FY2002* reported that $44.802 billion was requested for combating terrorism (both defensive and offensive measures for homeland security, overseas budget, and against conventional weapons and weapons of mass destruction) for FY2003.[1] Of this, about $2.905 billion – or 5.5% of the total – was requested for federal R&D to develop technologies to deter, prevent or mitigate terrorist acts. This is an increase from FY2002, when appropriated funds, combined with the Emergency Response Fund, totaled $36.468 billion, with R&D funding at $1.162 billion, or 3.2% of the total. The budget request for FY2003 Counterterrorism R&D is about double the amount appropriated for FY2002; funding for FY2002 was about triple the amount allocated in FY2001. The three largest funding increases for FY2003 were for the Department of Health and Human Services (DHHS), the Environmental Protection Agency (EPA), and the National Science Foundation (NSF). See Table 1. OSTP has identified some examples of the

---

[1] OMB, *Annual Report to Congress on Combating Terrorism, FY2002,* June 2002, authorized by Congress in Section 1051 of the FY1998 National Defense Authorization Act, P.L. 105-85 (which required information on executive branch funding to combat terrorism) and section 1403 of P.L. 105-26 (which required information on domestic preparedness), p. 15. See also: President George W. Bush, *Securing the Homeland, Strengthening the Nation,* 2002.

Administration's science and technology-related antiterrorism priorities for FY2003.[2]

As shown in Table 1, the *Department of Health and Human Service (DHHS),* with 57% of the total, would be the largest supporter of federal Counterterrorism R&D, reflecting the Administration's emphasis on bioterrorism. In previous years, the largest recipient of such funding was the national security community. DHHS would receive an increase of $1.65 billion, for a total of about $ 1.77 billion requested in FY2003 for "NIH to research vaccines and other medicines for protection against bioterrorism."[3]

Funding for Counterterrorism R&D by the *national security community* at 25% of the total requested for FY2003, would go largely to the Defense Advanced Projects Agency (DARPA) in the Department of Defense (DOD), for war fighting applications as well as for bioterrorism.[4] The request included $420 million for DOD's Biological Counterterrorism Research Program, which would establish a Center for Biological Counterterrorism at the U.S. Army Medical Research and Materiel Command Fort Detrick, Maryland, and the Biological Defense Homeland Security Support Program, which would "initiate demonstration of technologies in two urban areas for the timely detection of bioterror events."[5] Other national security-related R&D would be for protection, contamination avoidance (including detection), and decontamination. The national security line also included $49 million for the Technical Support Working Group (TSWG) – a State Department/DOD "interagency forum that identifies, prioritizes, and coordinates interagency and international R&D requirements for combating terrorism" and conducts R&D specifically to develop new technologies and equipment for counterterrorism. In recent years, about 20 to 25% of TSWG's funding has come from other agencies.[6] (TSWG's functions are discussed in more detail below in the sections entitled "Current Organization for Counterterrorism R&D" and "Creative R&D Funding Mechanisms.")

---

[2] The website is [http://www.ostp.gov/html/AntiTerrorismS&T.pdf].
[3] OMB, *Annual Report to Congress on Combating Terrorism, FY2002,* pp. 17-18.
[4] OMB, *Annual Report to Congress on Combating Terrorism, FY2002,* p. 27.
[5] OMB, *Annual Report to Congress on Combating Terrorism, FY2002,* p. 27.
[6] OMB, *Annual Report to Congress on Combating Terrorism, FY2002,* p. 28.

Table 1. Research and Development Funding to Combat Terrorism, by Agency, FY2000-FY2003 (Request) (Dollars in Millions)

Agency	FY2000 Actual	FY2001 Actual	FY2002 Enacted	FY2002 Emergency Response Fund	FY2003 Request
Agriculture	$37.3	$51.7	$83.9	$91.3	$48.4
Commerce	9.6	0	6.3	0	20.0
Energy	59.7	66.2	64.9	19.0	99.8
Environmental Protection Agency	not available	0	2.8	1.5	75.0
Department of Health and Human Services	109.7	102.8	119.1	180.0	1,770.9 (NIH, $1.75 bln; CDC, $40 mln and FDA, $50 mln).
Justice	45.2	11.4	66.1	0	36.1
National Science Foundation	not available	7.0	7.0	0	27.0
National Security	190.0	298.9	385.5	11.0	767.2
Transportation	50.7	50.2	58.3	64.0	59.3
Treasury	2.1	1.2	1.1	0	1.1
Total	$511.3	$589.4	$795.2	$366.8	$2,905.23

Source: OMB, *Annual Report to Congress on Combating Terrorism, FY2001*, p. 27 for column labeled FY2000. The rest of the data is from: OMB, *Annual Report to Congress on Combating Terrorism, June 24, 2002*, p. 26.

(Some of the data presented by OMB appears to conflict internally and also with agency-generated information. For example, the *OMB Annual Report to Congress on Combating Terrorism, FY2002* reported that the DOD counterterrorism R&D budget request for FY2003 would be $835 million (p. 66); whereas the total "national security" R&D budget request which includes DOD, reports the DOD budget request at $767.2 million (p. 26). As another example, DOD's Chemical and Biological Defense Program request for FY2003, according to congressional testimony, totaled $1.329 billion, of which $933 million would go to research, development, test, and evaluation (RDT&E). This is about $300 million more than in the President's budget request. Of this amount reported by DOD, $576 million was for S&T base and $436 million for procurement.[7] For additional details see below in Appendix 2, in the section on "FY2003 Bioterrorism R&D Priorities.")

The Environmental Protection Agency's budget for counterterrorism R&D was to be increased by $72.2 million in FY2003 for research for better techniques for cleaning up buildings contaminated by biological agents and

[7] Dale S. Klein, "Biological Terrorism: Department of Defense Research and Development," Testimony before the Emerging Threats and Capabilities Subcommittee of the Senate Armed Services Committee, at a hearing on *Technology for Combating Terrorism and Weapons of Mass Destruction (WMD)*, Apr. 10, 2002, p. 2.

for work on the effects of World Trade Center dust contaminants on human health.

The *Department of Energy's* (DOE) counterterrorism R&D has ranged across such areas as genomic sequencing, development of new DNA-based diagnostics, advanced modeling and simulation, and microfabrication technologies. DOE "is developing models for evaluating effectiveness of response and mitigation measures, such as reducing vulnerability of installations and improving operations and procedures at key urban facilities (e.g. evacuation, sheltering, traffic control, train control in subways, control of air handling systems)."[8] DOE also supports counterterrorism R&D at federal laboratories, R&D to improve the security of federal laboratories, and systems R&D totaling $20 million for the National Infrastructure Simulation and Analysis Center. DOE's laboratories' counterterrorism budgets have increased. Before the September 11 attacks, Sandia and Lawrence Livermore National Laboratories had done work relating to materials used in weapons of mass destruction, focusing largely on nuclear weapons. After the attacks, work accelerated on assessing anthrax detection and treatment activities for the Postal Service and congressional buildings, and taking atmospheric measurements to detect possible airborne toxic agents.[9] DOE's National Nuclear Security Administration (NNSA) R&D program "emphasizes maintaining the technology base and conducting the applied research needed to develop and demonstrate nuclear, chemical, and biological detection and related technologies…."[10]

The *Department of Agriculture's* (USDA) Agricultural Research Service conducts counterterrorism-related research into plant, pest, and animal diseases from natural or inadvertent introductions. The *Department of Justice's* R&D focuses on technologies for law enforcement efforts against terrorism. In the *Commerce Department,* R&D at the National Institute of Standards and Technology. (NIST), focuses on protecting information systems with attention to "system survivability and cryptography...."

National Science Foundation counterterrorism R&D supports combating bioterrorism in the areas of infectious diseases and microbial genome sequencing;[11] and critical infrastructure protection R&D, including $204 million requested for basic research on encryption technologies, energy processing systems, computing reliability, remediation robotics and

[8] OMB, *Annual Report to Congress on Combating Terrorism, FY2001,* p. 36.
[9] Kerry Boyd, "National Laboratories Accelerate Counterterrorism Efforts," *GovExec.com,* Apr. 22, 2002.
[10] OMB, *Annual Report to Congress on Combating Terrorism, FY2002,* p. 28.
[11] OMB, *Annual Report to Congress on Combating Terrorism, FY2002,* pp. 17-18.

modeling and simulation. It also funds Disaster Response Research Teams and a Cybercorp Scholarship program to support graduate students studying information technology who plan to work for the government (FY2003 funding requested at $11 million).[12]

Many agencies have posted lists of research opportunities for counterterrorism R&D. Centralized access to these is available from a National Association of State Universities and Land-Grant Colleges/Association of American Universities (NASULGC) website at [http://www.aau.edu/resources/research.html].[13]

---

[12] *OMB, Annual Report to Congress on Combating Terrorism, FY2002*, p. 65.

[13] Includes links to *Research Opportunities, NIAID Bioterrorism Research Agenda*, Mar. 14, 2002; *National Security Education Program Institutional Grants FY2002 Counter-Terrorism R&D; The National Science Foundation Response to Terrorist Attacks, Federal Technical Support Working Group (TSWG) Broad Agency Announcements*, Mar. 2002; *Department of Defense; National Institute of Mental Health; National Institutes of Health -Bioterrorism Research Funding Opportunities.*

Chapter 3

ADMINISTRATION PRIORITIES AND STRATEGY FOR HOMELAND SECURITY-RELATED R&D

The Administration has taken steps to develop priorities for counterterrorism R&D. This is reflected in budget priority documents, strategy documents released by the Office of Homeland Security (OHS), and activities undertaken by Antiterrorism Task Force Working Groups, which are part of the National Science and Technology Council (NSTC).

OSTP and OMB have identified the Administration's FY2004 budget priorities for "Homeland Security and Antiterrorism R&D" as follows:

> ... [E]nhancing our capabilities for (a) early detection of catastrophic terrorist threats and any subsequent exposures, (b) rapid response to them and mitigation of their effects, and (c) physical decontamination techniques and prophylactic and treatment measures. Research should be focused on areas with the potential to dramatically enhance our capabilities for detecting the presence of, and responding to, nuclear, biological, chemical, radiological, and conventional explosive threats in air, sea, rail, and road transport, both beyond and within our borders. Other priority areas include advances in information technology for examining large and disparate databases to identify any anomalies that might indicate terrorist intent on the part of individuals or groups of individuals, and the development of better biometric techniques, applied at the phenotype or genotype levels, for verifying or determining terrorist identity. Additionally, this effort should identify and apply relevant computer and network security research, including research developed under NITRD [Networking and Information Technology R&D, another interagency R&D priority]. ...Agency budget

requests in these areas should factor in recommendations of the President's Critical Infrastructure Protection Standing Committee for Research and Development.[14]

In addition to these budget emphases, in July 2002, OHS released a comprehensive *National Strategy for Homeland Security* that identified goals for many areas, including science and technology. See Table 2.

Table 2. Summary of the Major Science and Technology Initiatives in the OHS Document, National Strategy for Homeland Security

- *Develop chemical, biological, radiological, and nuclear countermeasures*
- *Develop systems for detecting hostile intent*
- *Apply biometric technology to identification devices*
- *Improve the technical capabilities of first responders*
- *Establish a mechanism for rapidly producing prototypes*
- *Conduct demonstrations and pilot deployments*
- *Set standards for homeland security technology*
- *Establish a system for high-risk, high-payoff homeland security research.*[15]

It has also been reported that separate agencies will prepare strategic plans to address homeland security issues. For instance, reportedly, the EPA plan will include a review of the capacity of its laboratories to transport and detect samples of toxic agents.[16] The Administration plans to announce a "comprehensive plan for defending the nation against biological warfare," according to Anna Johnson-Winegar, Deputy Assistant Secretary of Defense for chemical and biological defense. Among the R&D topics to be considered is the creation a national vaccine strategy and office to oversee the development of vaccines to fight diseases.[17] In addition, as noted below,

---

[14] Memorandum for the Heads of Executive Departments and Agencies, From John H. Marburger, III, Director, OSTP and Mitchell Daniels, Director, OMB, *FY2004 Interagency Research and Development Priorities,* May 30, 2002 [http://www.ostp.gov/html/ombguidmemo.pdf].

[15] Office of Homeland Security, (EOP), *National Strategy for Homeland Security,* July 2002, p. 52-54

[16] Pat Phibbs, "Strategic Plan on Homeland Security to Emerge in Summer, EPA Official Says," *Daily Report for Executives,* May 16, 2002, p A-6.

[17] Neil Munro, "Bioterrorism Preparedness Plan Expected this Summer," *GovExec.com,* May 3, 2002.

the five NSTC Antiterrorism working groups are preparing lists of priorities for counter terrorism R&D that will be used in developing detailed FY2004 budget requests. (See Appendix 1.)

Chapter 4

CURRENT ORGANIZATION FOR INTERAGENCY COORDINATION OF COUNTERTERRORISM R&D

Proposals to improve coordination of Counterterrorism R&D received considerable attention from expert commissions and groups before the terrorist attacks of September 11, 2001.[18] These groups noted that such R&D often was underfunded, not well-prioritized or developed within programs for short-term and longer-term fundamental research. Often R&D was fragmented across many departments or was wastefully duplicated, not clearly related to security requirements as defined by intelligence agencies, and poorly positioned to ensure rapid transitioning into technology, testing, and procurement. These groups recommended that linkages with the academic and industrial sectors be strengthened to take advantage of leading-edge work. Before the September 2001 attacks, the most prominent coordination groups for Counterterrorism R&D were the Technical Support Working Group, the National Security Council, the Office of Science and Technology Policy, and the National Science and Technology Council. Since then Counterterrorism R&D functions in these units have been augmented and the Office of Homeland Security was created and tasked with some R&D coordination functions.

Discussed next are organizational arrangements for Counterterrorism R&D, exclusive of those in OSTP. These are summarized in Table 3.

---

[18] See the summary of information about these reports in CRS Report RL31202, *Federal Research and Development for Counter Terrorism: Organization, Funding, and Options*, January 3, 2002, throughout and especially pp. 8-10.

TECHNICAL SUPPORT WORKING GROUP (TSWG)

Before September 11, 2001, the most visible part of the federal apparatus for coordinating the planning and conduct of interagency Counterterrorism R&D was the Technical Support Working group (TSWG), which operates under the policy guidance of the Department of State-chaired Interagency Group on Terrorism. Its activities have been intensified since the attacks.[19] TSWG identifies, prioritizes, and coordinates interagency and international R&D for combating terrorism. It is mostly "...focused on near-term, requirements-driven, non-medical R&D with a focus on deployable technologies that will serve the needs of first responders."[20] It provides "a way for technologies to be developed when a single agency cannot invest sufficiently in a technology that would benefit multiple agencies ...." TSWG coordinated $60 million worth of R&D in FY2000.[21] This constituted what GAO called "... a minor share of all terrorism-related research and development being conducted across the federal government...."[22] As noted above, funding for TSWG was requested at $49 million for FY2003. About

[19] On October 23, 2001, the TSWG issued a broad agency announcement (BAA) request – a special method DOD uses to place a contract to procure information or adapt existing technology rapidly and with less red tape than is typical. (Under Secretary of Defense for Acquisition, Technology and Logistics and Combating Terrorism Technology Support Office, Technical Support Working Group, *Broad Agency Announcement BAA 02-Q-4655,* Oct. 23, 2001, p. 16.) DOD was seeking information to develop 38 specific Counterterrorism technologies for military, intelligence, and security operations that could be deployed within the rapid time frame of 12 to 18 months. (See Greg Schneider and Robert O'Hare, "Pentagon Makes Rush Order for Anti-Terror Technology," *Washington Post,* Oct. 26, 2001, p. A10.) Among the technologies and systems DOD sought were an automated system to use voice prints to locate and track terrorist suspects; a speaker recognition system to identify Middle Eastern and Central/South Asian languages in speech; a battery-powered device to analyze liquid samples for the presence of biological warfare agents; and walkthrough portals for nonstationary personnel screening (BAA 02-Q-4655, pp. 17-23). This announcement generated more than 12,000 proposals which could possibly result in awards during FY2002 totaling $20 million to $40 million. ("Industry Submits 12,000 Proposals to Help in U.S. Fight Against Terrorism," *Daily Report for Executives,* Jan. 15, 2002, A-l.) The TSWG issued two additional BAAs on March 4, 2002, (DAAD 05-02-T-0215) which focused on "Chemical, Biological, Radiological and Nuclear Countermeasures," and "Investigative Support and Forensics." Announcements issued in July 2002 solicited proposals for technologies dealing with "Explosives Detection," "Improved Device Defeat," "Infrastructure Protection," "Personnel Protection," "Physical Security," and "Tactical Operations Support." (BAA 02-Q-4702 and 02-Q-4738, issued on July 22, 2002. BAAs are accessible from https://www.bids.tswg.gov/tswg/bids.nsf/Main?OpenFrameset&589 PCV.)

[20] Letter from Robin Cleveland, National Security Programs, OMB, to Stephen Caldwell, GAO, Sept. 4, 2001, in GAO, *Combating Terrorism: Selected Challenges and Related Recommendations,* Sept. 2001 (GAO-01-822), p. 163.

[21] GAO, *Combating Terrorism,* September 2001, p. 82.

[22] GAO, *Combating Terrorism,* September 2001, p. 82.

2/3 of TSWG's funding is from national security agencies and an additional 1/3 comes from some of the more than 40 other agencies that participate in its activities.

Table 3. Summary of Interagency Coordination for Counterterrorism R&D, Other Bodies, Including Office of Homeland Security

National Security Council (NSC)

- Preparedness Against Weapons of Mass Destruction Group
  - Subgroup on R&D (chaired by OSTP; TSWG is a member)

Office of Homeland Security (OHS)

- Homeland Security Council (HSC)
- Policy Coordinating Committee (PCC) on Research and Development, led by OSTP Assistant Director for National Security
- PCC on Public Health Preparedness
- Homeland Security Advisory Council
  - Senior Advisory Committees (includes PCAST members)

Technical Support Working Group (TSWG) (Coordinates and funds R&D for technologies to combat terrorism that are useful to more than one agency; headed by Dept. of State and Dept. of Defense)

Source: Prepared by CRS

TSWG also addresses joint international operational requirements through cooperative R&D with the United Kingdom, Canada, and Israel, and has an outreach program, so that state and local agencies can benefit from new technology developments. The group operates under the "technical oversight of the DOD Office of the Assistant Secretary of Defense for Special Operations and Low-Intensity Conflict. An Executive Committee chaired by the Department of State representative provides program direction. Members of the Executive Committee include representatives from DOD, DOE, and the Department of Justice (FBI)." DOD manages and executes the programs through the Combating Terrorism Technology Support Office.[23] TSWG has eight subgroups that focus on developing technology and prototyping efforts.[24] Each subgroup has many federal agency members, for instance, the Chemical and Biological Weapons

---

23 GAO, *Combating Terrorism,* September 2001, pp. 79-82.

24 Technical Support Working Group, *Program Overview 2000: Technical Support Working Group,* passim, preface, and p. 37. The TSWG subgroups deal with: chemical, biological, radiological, and nuclear countermeasures; explosive detection; improvised device defeat; infrastructure protection; investigative support and forensics; personnel protection; physical security surveillance, collection, and operations support; and tactical operations support [http://www.tswg.gov/tswg/home.htm].

(CBW) group membership numbers 15 major departments and agencies and many subunits within agencies.

NATIONAL SECURITY COUNCIL (NSC)

The National Security Council (NSC) has core responsibility to coordinate defense and foreign policy-related counterterrorism R&D policy across the government. It has a Policy Coordinating Committee on Counterterrorism and National Preparedness and a NSC-chaired Preparedness against Weapons of Mass Destruction Group (PWMD), with eight subgroups, including a Research and Development Subgroup, which reports to the NSC chair. The PWMD group was chartered under National Security Presidential Decision Directive-1, dated February 2001, to address the government's preparedness to forestall or respond to terrorist incidents involving weapons of mass destruction (chemical, biological, radiological or nuclear). "All federal departments and agencies with interests, equities, or needs in research and development for combating terrorism are represented on the PWMD R&D Subgroup."[25] The subgroup works to coordinate ongoing R&D activities and to assist in the preparation and review of the President's budget request for work on counterterrorism R&D and it makes recommendations to the PWMD. It is chaired by OSTP; a TSWG co-chair is a member of the Subgroup. While TSWG focuses on shorter term projects only of interest to its members, the NSC subgroup focuses on long-range projects and "... has a broad role in identifying long-range, large-scale research and development issues that involve preventing, countering, and responding to chemical, biological, radiological, or nuclear terrorist attacks." The PWMD R&D subgroup consults "with other NSC subgroup chairs to identify comprehensive R&D needs in preparedness for combating terrorism; identifying and prioritizing R&D gap-filling objectives; implementing a process for reporting progress toward achieving R&D objectives; and continuing the ongoing effort to achieve concordance of R&D objectives with agency programs."[26]

---

[25] Letter Cleveland to Caldwell, in GAO, *Combating Terrorism,* p. 164.
[26] Letter Cleveland to Caldwell, in GAO *Combating Terrorism,* p. 165.

OFFICE OF HOMELAND SECURITY (OHS)

On October 8, 2001 the President established the Office of Homeland Security (OHS) by Executive Order 13228, and named Governor Tom Ridge the Assistant to the President for Homeland Security. The OHS, located in the Executive Office of the President, has the "mission to develop and coordinate the implementation of a comprehensive national strategy to secure the United States from terrorist threat or attacks. The Office was directed to coordinate the executive branch's efforts to detect, prepare for, prevent, protect against, respond to, and recover from terrorist attacks...."[27] Also, it would advise the Director of the Budget on programs that will contribute to the Administration's strategy. Although the Assistant for Homeland Security can review the budgets of homeland security-related programs submitted to the OMB and suggest legislation to help agencies fight terrorism, he has no authority to modify or approve agency budgets. The executive order creating the Office of Homeland Security did not include either R&D priority-setting or R&D coordination among the functions assigned to it, which included such things as "detection," "response and recovery," "prevention," and "incident management." However, the office was assigned activities that explicitly or implicitly involve applications of science and technology.[28]

---

[27] "President Establishes Office of Homeland Security, Summary of the President's Executive Order, The Office of Homeland Security and the Homeland Security Council," White House Press Release, Oct. 8, 2001.

[28] For instance, with respect to "detection," it was given responsibility to coordinate activities to ensure that agencies have sufficient technological capabilities to collect intelligence data about terrorism, and to coordinate development of monitoring protocols and equipment for use in detecting the release of biological, chemical, and radiological hazards. Under the function of "preparedness," it was tasked to coordinate national efforts to ensure public health preparedness, including stockpiling of vaccine and Pharmaceuticals and hospital capacity. Under the function of "protection," the office was to coordinate efforts to protect critical infrastructure, including energy, telecommunications, nuclear materials, transportation, agriculture, food and water systems, and access to, and use of, chemical, biological, radiological, nuclear, explosive or other materials. It was also assigned, as part of its "response and recovery" functions, coordination of containment and removal of biological, chemical, radiological, explosive or other hazardous materials. (Executive Order Establishing Office of Homeland Security and the Homeland Security Council, Oct. 8, 2001.)

Homeland Security Council's Policy Coordination Committee

In addition to creating the Office of Homeland Security, Executive Order 13228 created a Homeland Security Council, whose purpose is to advise and assist the "President with respect to all aspects of homeland security." The Council is to "serve as the mechanism for ensuring coordination of homeland security-related activities of executive departments and agencies and effective development and implementation of homeland security policies."[29] The Director of the Office of Science and Technology Policy was neither named a member of the Homeland Security Council, nor mentioned among the specific department and agency heads who would be "invited to attend Council meetings pertaining to their responsibilities."[30]

Homeland Security Presidential Directive-1 regarding the "Organization and Operation of the Homeland Security Council," released on October 30, 2001, created a "Homeland Security Council Principals Committee," – as the "senior interagency forum under the Homeland Security Council."[31] Also established at this time was a Homeland Security Council Deputies Committee (HSC/DC) to serve as the senior sub-Cabinet interagency forum for consideration of policy issues affecting homeland security. The OSTP Director was not named to these groups.

Under the directive, eleven "Policy Coordination Committees" (PCC) were attached to the Homeland Security Council Office to provide interagency coordination for the development and implementation of homeland security policies by multiple federal departments and agencies and

[29] Executive Order Establishing Office of Homeland Security and the Homeland Security Council, Oct. 8, 2001.

[30] "President Establishes Office of Homeland Security." *White House Press Release,* Oct. 8, 2001.

[31] The OSTP Director was not named a member of the Principals Committee. The members are the Secretaries of the Treasury, of Defense, of Health and Human Services, and of Transportation; the Attorney General, the Director of OMB, the Assistant to the President for Homeland Security, the Assistant to the President and Chief of Staff; the Director of Central Intelligence; the Director of the Federal Bureau of Investigation, the Director of FEMA; the Assistant to the President and Chief of Staff to the Vice President. The Assistant to the President for National Security Affairs shall be invited to attend all meetings. The following people are to be invited to the committee meetings when issues pertaining to their responsibilities and expertise are discussed: the Secretaries of State, of the Interior, of Agriculture, of Commerce, of Labor, of Energy, and of Veterans Affairs, the Administrator of the EPA, and the Deputy National Security Advisor for Combating Terrorism. The Counsel to the President may also be invited. Other heads of departments and agencies and senior officials shall be invited, when appropriate.

to coordinate those policies with State and local government. The committees also are to provide "policy analysis for consideration by the more senior committees of the HSC system...." Members "shall include representatives from the executive departments, offices and agencies represented in the HSC/DC" of which the OSTP is not a member. One PCC deals with "research and development," and was to be chaired by a senior director from the Office of Homeland Security.[32]

OFFICE OF SCIENCE AND TECHNOLOGY POLICY (OSTP)

The Office of Science and Technology Policy (OSTP) in the Executive Office of the President (EOP), was established statutorily in 1976[33] to provide the President with advice on science and technology (S&T) issues. The law authorized OSTP to be headed by a director, who is presidentially nominated and confirmed by the Senate. The OSTP Director may be named as the President's Science and Technology Advisor. From time to time Presidents have named their science advisor an assistant to the President. This is not mandatory nor statutorily required. The current OSTP Director, Dr. John Marburger, was not named an assistant to the President or science advisor to the President. OSTP has its own federally funded research and development center (FFRDC), the Science and Technology Policy Institute (STPI), currently contracted to the RAND corporation, to conduct policy analyses and provide other support.

Except for its NSC committee responsibilities, before September 11, 2001, OSTP did not have specific counterterrorism R&D functions. Expert group recommendations were made before then to expand OSTP's role. GAO recommended that "to reduce duplication and leverage resources, ... the Assistant to the President for Science and Technology."[34] [who, in the past, has been the Director of the Office of Science and Technology Policy], "[should]... develop a strategic plan for research and development to combat terrorism, coordinating this with federal agencies and state and local authorities." GAO said this should be coordinated with the national strategy

---

[32] "Homeland Security Presidential Directive-1, Subject: Organization and Operation of the Homeland Security Council," October 29, 2001.

[33] Title II of P.L. 94-282 (National Science and Technology Policy, Organization, and Priorities Act of 1976.)

[34] As pointed out, P.L. 94-282, did not create such an "assistant."

to combat terrorism that would have its focal point in the Executive Office of the President.[35]

The U.S. Commission on National Security/21st Century (the Hart-Rudman Commission), that was convened by the Secretary of Defense, reported in *Road Map for National Security: Imperative for Change the Phase III Report,* February 15, 2001.[36] It focused on actions to strengthen national security capability broadly (without focusing specifically on counterterrorism). The commission recommended creating a cabinet-level National Homeland Security Agency (NHSA) with responsibility for planning, coordinating and integrating various U.S. government activities involved in homeland defense. Federal R&D resources, it said, should be doubled to strengthen the science base as a general national security defense. The Commission urged that OSTP play a paramount role in collecting data about R&D, in developing policies to strengthen the science base, and that the "president should empower his Science Advisor to establish non-military R&D objectives that meet changing national needs, and to coordinate budget development within the relevant departments and agencies." It also recommended that the National Science and Technology Council (NSTC), the interagency coordinating group managed by OSTP, should be strengthened to help identify additional creative, targeted large-scale governmental scientific and technological initiatives in key fields.[37]

OSTP's Evolving Responsibilities for Counterterrorism R&D

(See Table 4.) Dr. Marburger testified that after the terrorist attacks, the NSC's PCC on Preparedness Against Weapons of Mass Destruction, which OSTP chairs, "... initiated briefings from agencies on their bioterrorism-related R&D programs and on specific projects ... for detecting and tracking threats."[38] Meetings with federal agencies, he said, typically included representatives of the OMB, OHS, Domestic Policy Council, Office of the

---

[35] GAO, *Combating Terrorism,* p. 87.

[36] U.S. Commission on National Security/21st *Road Map for National Security: Imperative for Change, the Phase III Report,* February 15, 2001, p. 30, Century (the Hait-Rudman Commission, convened by the Secretary of Defense).

[37] Hart-Rudman report, p. 34.

[38] Statement of Hon. John H. Marburger, "Science of Bioterrorism: Is the Federal Government Prepared?" Hearing before the House Committee on Science, Dec. 5, 2001. See also: "An Interview with John Marburger: Terrorism, Money, Contacts Top Science Adviser's Agenda," *Science*, Nov. 23, 2001.

Vice President, and Cabinet Affairs.[39] During April 2002 hearings, Dr. Marburger testified that in order to coordinate counterterrorism R&D, OSTP interacts with relevant federal agencies as well as with "Congress ... the science community, the private sector and higher education."[40] OSTP sought advice from the National Academies and from its own federally funded R&D center, specifically to develop a taxonomy and inventory of agency activities in "antiterrorism R&D" with the objective of identifying "gaps, duplication, and opportunities for collaboration."[41] See Appendix 4 for a summary of the report the National Academies prepared to help the government define counterterrorism R&D priorities and organizational arrangements.

After his confirmation, the new OSTP Director eliminated two of the divisions that had existed previously – the divisions of national security and of environment – on the grounds that the office was too fragmented.[42] At least one critic, an official of the American Association for the Advancement of Science, is reported to have said that "eliminating the national security position 'is a big blow' to forging links to the powerful National Security Council... [on terrorism issues]."[43]

---

[39] Marburger Testimony, Dec. 5, 2001.

[40] Statement of Hon. John H. Marburger, III, Director of the OSTP, before the Subcommittee on Emerging Threats and Capabilities, Committee on Armed Services, U.S. Senate, Apr. 10, 2002.

[41] Interviews with OSTP staff. See also Hafner, Apr. 11, 2002, and Steve Bunk, "Science and Homeland Security," *The Scientist,* July 8, 2002.

[42] David Malakoff and Robert Koenig, "Counterterrorism: U.S. Science Agencies Begin to Lend a Hand," *Science,* Oct. 26, 2001, pp. 761-762; Chris Mooney, "Political Science: The Bush Administration Snubs Its Science Adviser," *American Prospect,* December 3, 2001.

[43] Lawler, Andrew, "Marburger Shakes up White House Office," *Science,* Nov. 2, 2001, pp. 973-974.

Table 4. Summary of Interagency Coordination for Counterterrorism R&D, OSTP-related Responsibilities

Office of Science and Technology Policy (OSTP)

OSTP has been assigned responsibilities for:

- Immigration Policy (with DOS, DOD, DOE, DOEd, DOJ, FEMA); created IPASS
- Border Technology (with CIA and DOJ)
- Counter-Nuclear Smuggling Working Group (linked to OHS)

OSTP is also a member of:

- Non-Proliferation and Arms Control Technology Working Group, led by the Department of State,
- Counter Proliferation Program Review Committee, chaired by DOD, and
- Interagency group to develop guidelines for select agent regulations to be promulgated by DHHS and USDA in response to the passage of the Public Health Security and Bioterrorism Preparedness and Response Act, P.L. 107-188

OSTP's Assistant Director for National Security is also the OHS Senior Director for R&D

OSTP has relationships with the National Academies [of Science (NAS), Engineering (NAE), Institute of Medicine (IOM)]

OSTP's FFRDC (STPI) does counterterrorism work for it; it is run by RAND

National Science and Technology Council (NSTC) (managed by OSTP)

Antiterrorism Task Force, which has five working groups:

- Radiological, Nuclear and Conventional(RNC) Working Group (CIA, DOT, DOC, EPA, DOD, NSF, DOE, NSC, DOJ, NRC, DOS, OMB)
- Biological and Chemical Preparedness Working Group (DOD, HHS, CIA, DOC, DOE, DOT, EPA, NSF, USDA, DOJ/FBI, VA, STATE, DOI, NASA, Treasury, OMB, NSC, OHS, OSTP)
- Rapid Response Working Group (AFRRI, CDC, CIA, DARPA, DOD, DOEd, DOE, DOI, DOJ, DOT, EPA, FBI, FDA, FEMA, HHS, NASA, NOAA, NIC, NIOSH, NIST, NRC, NSF, OHS, OMB, OSHA, State, USDA, USPS, USSS, VA)
- Social, Behavioral and Education Sciences (SBE) Working Group (OSTP, NSF, NIH, DOD, DHHS, VA, NIJ, CDC, OHSA, and ED, with new members being added from the CIA, EPA, NIOSH, DARPA and FBI)
- Protection of Vulnerable Systems Working Group (connected to coordination efforts of the Special Advisor to the President for Cyber Space Security Richard Clarke. Together Clarke and Marburger co-chair a R&D Working Group focused on this issue)

President's Council of Advisors on Science and Technology (PCAST) (under OSTP)

Panel on Combating Terrorism (which is a member of the Senior Advisory Committee of the Homeland Security Advisory Council)

Not part of OSTP: *President's Critical Infrastructure Board* (The OSTP director is a member and co-chair of the R&D Subcommittee relating to information security.)

Source: Prepared by CRS.

President's Council of Advisors on Science and Technology (PCAST)

PCAST was originally established by President George Bush in 1990 to enable the President to receive advice from the private sector and academic community on technology, scientific research priorities, and math and science education.[44] The OSTP Director said he would utilize PCAST, which he co-chairs[45] for counterterrorism R&D advice. PCAST would be enlisted to assess issues such as "how to better mobilize the creativity and energy of private-sector technology companies in both preventing and responding to terrorism."[46] Subsequently the President charged PCAST with developing recommendations on "using S&T to combat terrorism"[47] via the PCAST Panel on the Science and Technology of Combating Terrorism. This subcommittee was to "examine the role of government to combat terrorism, identify obsolete regulations, and look at lessons learned by other nations that experience terrorism."[48] On July 23, 2002, PCAST released a draft report for public comment, entitled *Report on Maximizing the Contribution of Science and Technology within the New Department of Homeland Security.*[49] It focused on the organization, content, and operation of the R&D in a proposed Department of Homeland Security.

PCAST's Role in Homeland Security Advisory Council

On March 21, 2002, the President issued Executive Order 13260, entitled "Establishing the President's Homeland Security Advisory Council and Senior Advisory Committees for Homeland Security." Composed of 21 nonfederal (private and State and local government) members appointed by the President, its purpose is to advise the President through the Assistant for Homeland Security on a national strategy and specific strategies to secure the United States from terrorist threats or attacks and to recommend ways to

---

[44] The current version was created on September 30, 2001, when President George W. Bush signed Executive Order 13226.

[45] See also, Bara Vaida, "Bush High-Tech Council to Discuss Terrorism at First Meeting," *GovExec.com,* Dec. 12, 2001.

[46] Audrey T. Leath, "Positive Hearing for OSTP Director Nominee Marburger," *AIP Bulletin of Science Policy News,* Oct. 11, 2001.

[47] Richard M. Jones, "First Meeting of the President's Council of Advisors on Science and Technology," *FYI: The AIP Bulletin of Science Policy News,* Mar. 13, 2002.

[48] Jones, Mar. 13, 2002.

[49] Available at [http://www.ostp.gov/PCAST/DHSreport/html].

improve cooperation and cooperation among various sectors and information sources. Among its *ex officio* members are the Chair and the vice chair of the National Infrastructure Advisory Council; the Chairman of the President's National Security Telecommunications Advisory Committee; and the Chair of the PCAST's Panel on the Science and Technology of Combating Terrorism. Four senior advisory committees (SAC) are to deal with State and Local Officials; Academic and Policy Research; Private Sector; and Emergency Services, Law Enforcement and Public Health and Hospitals.[50]

FORMAL LINKS BETWEEN OHS AND OSTP

Formal links between the OHS and the OSTP include a staff member with dual responsibilities in each agency and the assignment of specific counterterrorism-related tasks to OSTP in cooperation with OHS. These interactions are discussed next.

Assistant OSTP Director Named Senior Director for R&D at OHS

Dr. Penrose (Parney) Albright was named to the positions of Assistant OSTP Director, National Security and Senior Director for Research and Development at the Office of Homeland Security and senior staff member for the PCC on R&D. Within OSTP, he reports to the OSTP Associate Director for Science. Dr. Albright is a Ph.D. physicist, with experience relating to ballistic and cruise missile defense. His most recent assignment before coming to OSTP was with DARPA, where he managed programs in hydrodynamic drag reduction, molecular biology, target tagging, and speech encoding. Before that he was with the Science and Technology Division of the Institute for Defense Analyses.[51] Albright's appointment, according to Dr. Marburger, will "'provide OHS seamless reach-back into the scientific talent resident in OSTP staff and [provides] OSTP awareness of the various issues OHS is confronting, while bringing the resources of the S&T

[50] "Homeland Security Council Executive Order," White House Press Release, Mar. 21, 2002 and "President Bust to Appoint the Following Individuals to Serve as Members of the President's Homeland Security Advisory Council," White House Press Release, June 11, 2002.

[51] Information provided by OSTP congressional liaison.

community to bear on homeland security issues in an efficient and timely manner....'"[52]

OSTP Responsibilities Relating to Counter-terrorism, Student Visas and Immigration

During fall 2001 the Assistant to the President for Homeland Security called upon the OSTP Director for scientific and technical advice, to provide some "science coordination"[53] dealing with the federal response relating to mail security and baggage inspection at airports,[54] and to identify counterterrorism experts in collaboration with the National Coordination Office for Information Technology R&D in the Commerce Department.[55] The OSTP Director was given responsibility to work in two specific R&D areas under Homeland Security Presidential Directive-2, that deals with "Combating Terrorism Through Immigration Policies," issued October 29, 2001. One was to develop, in cooperation with the Secretaries of State, Defense, Energy, and Education, and the Attorney General, and academic institutions, a program to "end the abuse of student visas and prohibit certain international students from receiving education and training in sensitive areas, including areas of study with direct application to the development and use of weapons of mass destruction."[56] This would involve identifying sensitive courses of study, identifying "problematic applicants" for student visas and denying their applications, and tracking students who receive a visa by looking at "the proposed major course of study, the status of the individual as a full-time student, the classes in which the student enrolls, and the source of the funds supporting the student's education."

A second responsibility mandated by Homeland Security Presidential Directive-2 required the OSTP Director, in conjunction with the Attorney General and the Director of Central Intelligence, to recommend methods and

---

[52] Marburger, Senate testimony, Apr. 10, 2002. See also: Lauren Hafner, "S&T Response to Emerging Anti-terror Needs Requires Flexibility, Senate Panel Hears," *Washington Fax*, Apr. 11, 2002.

[53] Mooney, Dec. 2001, op. cit., and "Terrorism, Money, Contacts Top Science Adviser's Agenda," *Science*, Nov. 23, 2001, p. 1642-1644.

[54] Statement of Hon. John H. Marburger, "Science of Bioterrorism: Is the Federal Government Prepared?" Hearing before the House Committee on Science, Dec. 5, 2001.

[55] Testimony at Hearing on the "Response of the Technology Sector in Times of Crisis," Senate Committee on Commerce, Science, and Transportation, Subcommittee on Science, Technology, and Space, Dec. 5, 2001.

[56] Section 3, "Abuse of International Student Status" in "Homeland Security Presidential Directive-2, Subject Combating Terrorism Through Immigration Policies," Oct. 29, 2001.

resources needed to use advanced technology to help enforce U.S. immigration laws by facilitating the identification of, and denying access to, aliens who are suspected of engaging in or supporting terrorist activity. Recommendations were also to be made about using existing databases to detect, identify, locate, and apprehend potential terrorists. The Director of OSTP was to submit to the Director of OMB proposed legislative remedies to overcome legal barriers to data sharing to achieve this objective. OSTP's Director was to make recommendations on technologies and associated budgetary requirements to the President through the Homeland Security Council.

Interagency Panel on Advanced Science Security

Part of OSTP's response to these tasks consisted of its coordination of much of the work of an interagency working group which refined guidelines regarding student immigration and courses of study,[57] resulting in development of an Administration plan released on May 7, 2002. The White House plan proposed creating an Interagency Panel on Advanced Science Security (IPASS) to screen foreign graduate students and scientists who apply for visas to study sensitive subjects at U.S. colleges and universities. IPASS will be tasked with guarding access to "unique and sensitive" U.S. education or training that could be used against us or our allies. It will be composed of representatives from major U.S. science agencies, as well as officials from the Departments of State, Justice and Commerce. Co-chairs of the IPASS will be appointed by the Secretary of State and the Attorney General. Reportedly, a presidential directive is being prepared which will define how IPASS will operate.[58] Plans are for visa applications to be screened according to the nationality of the student, his or her educational background, area of study, and the nature of any research being conducted at the institution. An OSTP official said that, "The current State Department Technology Alert List of 16 broad categories already designated to trigger additional inquiry on visa applications[59] is a starting point of the list of

---

[57] Diana Jean Scheme, "A Nation Challenged: Imitation Rules; Plans on Foreign Students Worry College Officials," *New York Times,* Apr. 18, 2002. Conversation with Dr. Penrose Albright, OSTP, Apr. 2002.

[58] Jeffrey Mervis, "U.S. Antiterrorism: Panel Would Screen Foreign Scholars," *Science,* May 17, 2002, pp. 1213-1215.

[59] Pursuant to Section 212 of the Immigration and Nationality Act as amended, State Department consular officials who issue student visas abroad are supposed to deny visas for U.S. study in sensitive fields and/or areas of illegal export of technology. The areas

'unique and sensitive' S&T areas IPASS will consider ...."[60] Reportedly, a new list will be developed in cooperation with U.S. educational institutions. While most U.S. educators seem pleased with the creation of the panel, they say they felt excluded from discussions about establishing it and expect to be asked to participate in panel deliberations in the future.[61]

OSTP's Responsibilities Relating to Cyber-security R&D

Executive Order 13231, issued October 16, 2001, gave the OSTP Director a third responsibility, related to cyber-security R&D. As is described further in Appendix 3 on "Information Security R&D," the Special Advisor to the President for Cyber Space Security, is also the Chairman of the President's Critical Infrastructure Board and reports both to the NSC and the OHS. He was required to coordinate with the OSTP Director to develop a federal R&D program to protect "information systems for critical infrastructure."[62] These activities are to be coordinated with NSC.

OSTP's Role in Other Groups

According to Dr. Marburger, "Working closely with OHS, an interagency working group called the "Counter-Nuclear Smuggling Working Group" has been created to develop a fully coordinated program for addressing the threat of nuclear smuggling across borders, both overseas and in the United States. This working group will develop a strategic plan with a unified set of program goals and priorities, including within its scope the programs that implement and deploy current capabilities, as well as

encompass 16 categories specified on the *Technology Alert List* to students from countries identified as "state sponsors of terrorism." The categories are: 1. Conventional Munitions, 2. Nuclear Technology, 3. Missile/missile Technology, 4. Aircraft and Missile Propulsion and Vehicular Systems, 5. Navigation and Guidance Control, 6. Chemical and Biotechnology Engineering, 7. Remote Imaging and Reconnaissance, 8. Advanced Computer/Microelectronic Technology, 9. Materials Technology, 10. Information Security, 11. Lasers and Directed Energy Systems, 13. Marine Technology, 14. Robotics, 15. Advanced Ceramics, 16. High Performance Metals and Alloys. (For additional details, see: "Visas Mantis,"[http://travel.state.gov/reciprocity/SAO/MANTIS.htm].)

60 Shirley Haley, "Bush Visa Screening Plan Incorporates S&T Agencies, Academic Community," *Washington Fax,* May 9, 2002.

61 Stephen Burd, "Bush May Bar Foreign Students From 'Sensitive Courses,'" *Chronicle of Higher Education,* Apr. 26, 2002.

62 "Critical Infrastructure Protection in the Information Age," Executive Order 13231, issued October 16, 2001.

programs that research and develop new capabilities. This group is co-chaired with the National Security Council and [works with]... the Office of Homeland Security's Research and Development Policy Coordinating Committee."[63]

Dr. Marburger testified that "OSTP also is engaged fully in such interagency groups as the Non-Proliferation and Arms Control Technology Working Group, led by the Department of State, and the Counter Proliferation Program Review Committee, chaired by the Department of Defense."[64] It also is participating in an interagency group to develop guidelines for select agent regulations to be promulgated by DHHS and USDA in response to the passage of the Public Health Security and Bioterrorism Preparedness and Response Act of 2002, P.L. 107-188.[65]

National Science and Technology Council (NSTC)

The National Science and Technology Council (NSTC) was established by Executive Order 12881 on November 23, 1993. This Cabinet-level council is the principal means for the President to coordinate science, space, and technology across the government. The President chairs the NSTC. Membership consists of the Vice President, the Assistant to the President for Science and Technology, who at times in the past has been the Director of the White House Office of Science and Technology Policy, cabinet secretaries and agency heads with significant science and technology responsibilities, and other White House officials. OSTP manages the activities of NSTC, which prepares R&D strategies for some topics and coordinates them across federal agencies.

NSTC's Committee on National Security (CNS) is charged with providing a formal mechanism for interagency policy review, planning, and coordination as well as the exchange of information regarding national security-related R&D. It was active during the Clinton Administration.[66] The

[63] Marburger, Senate testimony, Apr. 10, 2002.
[64] Marburger, Testimony, Apr. 10, 2002.
[65] Statement of John H. Marburger, Director, OSTP, Before the House Science Committee, June 27, 2002.
[66] Three Subcommittees and Interagency Working Groups were active during the last year of the Clinton Administration in 2000, including the Interagency Working Group on Critical Infrastructure Protection Research and Development, the Interagency Working Group on International Technology Transfer Issues and Policy, and the Interagency Working Group on Non-proliferation and Arms Control Technology.

NSTC's CNS has participated in "monitoring the research and development subgroup of the interagency Weapons of Mass Destruction Preparedness Group [PWMD subgroup of the National Security Council]. ...The CNS was briefed on and discussed the activities and progress of the R&D subgroup on several occasions."[67] GAO reported that neither the OSTP nor the NSTC's CNS have created a national R&D strategy to combat WMD-related terrorism and do not coordinate individual agency projects.[68] "As a result," the management of counterterrorism-related R&D is "self-governing and highly dependent on voluntary coordination mechanisms."[69]

The Committee on National Security appears to be inactive. The links, if any, between the NSTC's CNS and the National Security Council's PWMD R&D Subgroup and the CNS and the Homeland Security Council's Policy Coordination Committee for R&D have not been made known.

NSTC'S Antiterrorism Task Force

Shortly after the September 11, 2001 attacks the OSTP Director created a *Rapid Response Team* within the NSTC structure. The team draws on technical experts within relevant federal agencies to address critical time-sensitive technical issues. An example of this was OSTP's assembling of a technical team to assist the U.S. Postal Service in evaluating the effectiveness of various proposals for sanitizing mail contaminated with anthrax spores.[70] Also by spring 2002, OSTP's director had established an interagency Antiterrorism Task Force which incorporated the Rapid Response Team and also included other working groups dealing with

- Radiological, Nuclear and Conventional [Threats and Vulnerabilities],
- Biological and Chemical Preparedness, and
- Social, Behavioral and Education Sciences.

For a description of each of the groups' functions and members, see Appendix 1.

A separate NSTC *Protection of Vulnerable Systems* working group was created. It is "concerned with the nation's physical infrastructure and is

---

[67] *National Science and Technology Council, 2000 Annual Report,* http://www.ostp.gov/NSTC/html/nstc_ar.pdf.

[68] GAO, *Combating Terrorism,* p. 82.

[69] GAO, *Combating Terrorism,* p. 82.

[70] Marburger, Senate testimony, Apr. 10, 2002.

intimately connected with the coordination efforts of the Special Advisor to the President for Cyber Space Security Richard Clarke."[71]

OSTP is using these groups to conduct interagency reviews of federal R&D programs "... to assist agencies in determining which R&D efforts constitute the highest national priority items and should be integrated into their budgets, thereby reducing gaps and inefficiencies."[72] These activities also permit sharing of information about agencies' R&D program activities and outputs. Each working group had originally been directed to "set ... a five-year research agenda by August 1, 2002."[73] According to OSTP that information will be used in preparing the FY2004 budget request.[74]

[71] Marburger, Testimony, Apr. 10, 2002.

[72] OMB, *Annual Report to Congress on Combating Terrorism,* FY2002, p. 27.

[73] Marburger, Testimony, Apr. 10, 2002. Detailed information about the groups was provided by the OSTP congressional liaison staff.

[74] Interview, September 2002.

Chapter 5

PROPOSALS TO COORDINATE COUNTER-TERRORISM R&D IN A DEPARTMENT OR AGENCY

Some observers argue that the coordination mechanisms established in OSTP, OHS and other agencies as described above are inadequate. They say that fragmentation in priority-setting and the conduct of counterterrorism and homeland security R&D programs and policies imperils the nation's security. Core R&D priorities, they contend, should be set by a homeland security agency or department which would also have responsibility for managing the conduct of some R&D. Others disagree or urge caution when moving some R&D to a new department.

Even before the terrorist attacks, expert group recommendations were made to create a new counterterrorism agency, which would coordinate federal counterterrorism R&D. The Gilmore Commission recommended that the President should establish a statutorily authorized, cabinet-level National Office for Combating Terrorism in the Executive Office of the President. It would have five major sections, each headed by an assistant director. One section, that would focus on Research, Development, Test, and Evaluation (RDT&E) and National Standards, would develop a comprehensive plan for long-range research for combating terrorism, "provide direction and priorities for research and development and related test and evaluation ... for combating terrorism as well as for developing nationally recognized standards for equipment and laboratory protocols and techniques, with the ultimate objective being official certification."[75] It "would have budget and program and authority to review federal agency programs and budgets to ensure compliance with the priorities it established in the national strategy," [this is more budget approval authority than was granted to the Office of Homeland Security]; would coordinate national laboratory R&D to deal with terrorism, and would gather and disseminate information about off-the-shelf research and technology to combat terrorism.[76] The Commission recommended that the TSWG, which also serves "as an adjunct of the 'Interagency Working Group on Counterterrorism' under the National Security Council... become an adjunct to the National Office for Combating Terrorism in the same manner that it now serves in the NSC process and that it expand its coordination role for technical aspects of RDT&E for combating terrorism."[77] The commission also recommended a greater role for OSTP in setting federal R&D priorities and that the proposed Assistant Director for RDT&E and National Standards either enter into a formal relationship with OSTP or have appropriate members of the OSTP staff detailed to the Office for Combating Terrorism on a rotational basis.[78]

In June 2002, a National Academies' report observed that federal counterterrorism R&D was fragmented among agencies and that more interdisciplinary, cross-cutting work was needed. It recommended creation of a "federal office or agency with central responsibility for homeland security strategy and coordination and [that] ... this organization [should] have the structure and framework necessary to bring responsibility, accountability, and resources together to effectively utilize the nation's science and engineering capabilities." The report also supported creating a Homeland Security Institute to help set priorities and to provide technical capabilities and analysis, including test-bed evaluation, to support the organization. An Undersecretary for Technology was needed, "[t]o provide a focal point for guiding research and technology development programs across the department, and most importantly., engaging commitments from the major science, engineering, and medical science agencies that will remain outside the proposed new department."[79] The OSTP Director,

---

[75] Advisory Panel to Assess Domestic Response Capabilities for Terrorism Involving Weapons of Mass Destruction, *Toward a National Strategy for Combating Terrorism,* December 14, 2000, [second of three reports] Written in cooperation with the Rand Corporation, (Gilmore Commission Report, p. xi.)

[76] Gilmore report, pp. 37-38.

[77] Gilmore report, pp. 36-37.

[78] Gilmore report, pp. 37-38.

[79] Committee on Science and Technology for Countering Terrorism, National Research Council, *Making the Nation Safer: The Role of Science and Technology in Countering Terrorism,*

according to the report, should "lead an interagency process to develop the S&T research priorities for counterterrorism. These priorities should be responsive to, and aligned with, the overall counterterrorism agenda, developed by OHS and budget guidance should be promulgated to agencies to support their participation in appropriate programs."[80]

A draft report released in July 2002 by the President's Council of Advisors on Science and Technology (PCAST) recommended creating a DHS with an Under Secretary for Science and Technology with a variety of R&D responsibilities and a "Homeland Security federally funded research and development center (FFRDC)" ... to do systems analysis, support of systems engineering and "red teaming" ("the use of innovative individuals who emulate terrorists in selecting targets and planning attacks, based on simulation and controlled table-top and fielded exercises and tests"). It said that the DHS should also have laboratory and operational test and evaluation functions and a Homeland Security Advanced Research Agency to manage external R&D – primarily a funding conduit to industry and academia. PCAST also proposed that federal agency counterterrorism R&D activities be inventoried to assist Congress and DHS in identifying appropriate R&D responsibilities for DHS and gaps in coverage.[81]

In several documents released during the spring of 2002, the Administration made a case for including some R&D responsibilities in a homeland security department. These were represented in the Administration's *National Strategy for Homeland Security*, released in July 2002. It concluded,

> To date, research and development activities in support of homeland security have been underfunded, evolutionary, short-term in nature, fragmented across too many departments, and heavily reliant on spin-offs from the national security and medical sectors. Many of the involved agencies have little frontline knowledge of homeland security and little or no experience in technology acquisition and supporting research.[82]

It proposed creating a Department of Homeland Security which would coordinate homeland security R&D, create a centralized federal laboratory system R&D, and develop an independent analytical and evaluation

Washington, National Academy Press, 2002, pp. 12-6 and ES-17, [http://www.nap.edu/catalog/10415.html].

[80] *Making the Nation Safer...*, op. cit. p. 12-10.

[81] *Report on Maximizing the Contribution of Science and Technology Within the New Department of Homeland Security*, by The President's Council of Advisors on Science and Technology, July 23, 2002 [http://www.ostp.gov/PCAST/DHSreport.html].

[82] Available at [http://www.whitehouse.gov/homeland/book/index.html], p. 52

capability for testing of technologies.[83] Many of these proposals were subsequently incorporated into H.R. 5005. See below in the section entitled "Counterterrorism R&D Procurement, Analysis, or Evaluation Centers."

While some observers argue that core counterterrorism R&D should be consolidated in a homeland security department, others, such as the Brookings Institution in a July 15, 2002 report, *Assessing the Department of Homeland Security,* disagree or urge caution about moving some R&D to a new department. Brookings concluded that creation of a department should be deferred until the Administration's homeland security R&D strategy is more fully developed and that more attention should be given to prevention and R&D priorities that deal with controlling dangerous materials, sensors, surveillance and data management.[84]

[83] Source: [http://www.whitehouse.gov/homeland/book/index.html].

[84] Ivo H. Daadler, e. al., *Assessing the Department of Homeland Security,* Brookings, July 2002, p. viii and 28. Hereafter called "Brookings, July 2002."

Chapter 6

LEGISLATION TO AUTHORIZE A HOMELAND SECURITY OFFICE OR DEPARTMENT WITH R&D RESPONSIBILITIES

Some say that because the Office of Homeland Security was created by executive order and not by statute, Congress has little direct oversight of its activities, except for its authority to fund White House offices. Also, there has been criticism that since the OHS has no specific budgetary authority, it will not be able to effectively establish and coordinate policies and command other agencies, and that it does not share information and data with other agencies.[85]

Bills have been introduced in the 107th Congress to authorize both an OHS and to create a new department of homeland security, both with R&D coordination responsibilities.[86] The bills with the most legislative action are

---

[85] Rensselaer Lee, "Homeland Security Office: Issues and Options," May 20, 2002, CRS Report RL31421, 26 p.; David M. Walker, Comptroller General, *Homeland Security: Responsibility and Accountability for Achieving National Goals*, Testimony Before the Committee on Government Affairs, U.S. Senate, Apr. 11, 2002; Abraham McLaughlin, "With US on Alert, Ridge Lacks Clout," *Christian Science Monitor*, May 21, 2002; Molly M. Peterson, "Homeland Security Office a 'Toothless Tiger,' Senator Says," *GovExec.com*, Apr. 17, 2002; and Katherine McIntire Peters, "Lacking a Strategy Homeland Security Languishes," *GovExec.com*, Apr. 30, 2002.

[86] Two bills would create a homeland security office with R&D responsibilities. H.R. 3026, "Office of Homeland Security Act," introduced October 4, 2001 would establish an Office of Homeland Security within the Executive Office of the President, with a presidentially appointed, Senate-confirmed Director. Among other things, it would develop a homeland security strategy, including "a comprehensive research, development, and procurement

H.R. 5005, passed in the House, and S. 2452, under consideration in the Senate. Both bills would create homeland security departments, with an Under Secretary for Science and Technology and varying degrees of responsibility for counterterrorism science and technology.[87] S.2794 was introduced on July 25, 2002 and referred to the Senate Committee on Governmental Affairs. Many of its provisions are similar to the original proposal the President sent to Congress, introduced as H.R. 5005, that was amended before House passage.

H.R. 5005, "To Create a Department of Homeland Security"

On June 6, 2002, the President sent Congress a proposal for a Department of Homeland Security.[88] This was followed by legislation sent up to Congress and introduced June 24, 2002 as H.R. 5005. It differed somewhat from the organization outlined in the President's homeland security proposal document.[89] Following hearings and mark-up,[90] the House passed H.R. 5005 on July 26, 2002. The bill would create a Department of Homeland Security (DHS) with total R&D responsibilities estimated at $500 to $600 million, including $300 million for programs that would be newly authorized, according to the Congressional Budget Office (CBO).[91] See Table 5.

---

plan for supporting homeland security." H.R. 525, "Federal Office to Combat Terrorism Bill," would establish the President's Council on Domestic Preparedness, an interagency council chaired by the President, which among other things would require "An evaluation of available technologies and practices to determine the best means of protecting transportation, energy, and other infrastructure facilities against terrorist attacks."

[87] For a detailed comparison of these two bills, see: *Homeland Security: Side-by-Side Comparison of H.R. 5005 and S. 2452,107th Congress,* By Homeland Security Team Congressional Research Service, CRS Report RL31513.

[88] President George W. Bush, *The Department of Homeland Security,* June 6, 2002, 24 p.

[89] That original proposal would, among other things, have created different directorates and would have had responsibility for the support and conduct of some DHHS bioterrorism R&D and responsibilities for DOE laboratories.

[90] Funding for activities to be transferred under the original June 6 proposal totaled $37.5 billion, with a $3.4 billion R&D portfolio, according to AAAS. After some HHS programs were removed from the proposal, R&D programs in the H.R. 5005 as introduced reportedly would have totaled about $2.3 billion mostly from NIH. ("Proposed Dept. of Homeland Security Would Include NIH, DOE, and USDA R&D Programs," *AAAS R&D Funding Update,* June 21, 2002 [http://www.aaas.org/spp/rd/dhs0621.htm].)

[91] Congressional Budget Office, "Cost Estimate, July 23, 2002 on H.R. 5005, Homeland Security Act of 2002, As ordered reported by the Select Committee on Homeland Security

The existing OHS would continue in the Executive Office of the President; it is not clear if the existing OHS Homeland Security Council Policy Coordination Committee on R&D would continue.[92] The proposed DHS would have four operational units, each led by an Under Secretary: (1) Information Analysis and Infrastructure Protection; (2) Science and Technology; (3) Border and Transportation Security; and (4) Emergency Preparedness and Response. Most of DHS's research, development, test, and evaluation (RDT&E) functions would be under the jurisdiction of the Under Secretary for Science and Technology (created by Title III), who would have responsibility to fund and administer the agency's intramural and extramural research, development, test, and evaluation (RDT&E) with respect to developing countermeasures against chemical, biological, radiological, and nuclear weapons and other "emerging terrorist" threats (but not human health-related R&D); to establish a government-wide counterterrorism R&D strategy; and to coordinate with other agencies to eliminate duplication and fill unmet needs; and facilitate technology deployment.

The Under Secretary for Science and Technology would have responsibility for several Department of Energy (DOE) R&D programs to be transferred to DHS, excluding programs and activities relating to the U.S. strategic nuclear posture. DOE programs proposed for transfer include chemical and biological national security programs; some parts of the non-proliferation and verification R&D program directly relating to homeland security; nuclear smuggling; the nuclear assessment program of international materials protection and cooperation directly relating to homeland security; life sciences activities of the biological and environmental research program relating to microbial pathogens, computational gene sequencing technology development, and databases of microbial and other DNA sequence data; the advanced scientific computing research program at Lawrence Livermore National Laboratory; and the Environmental Measurements Laboratory. AAAS estimated the above DOE programs could total about $100 million.[93]

---

on July 19, 2002," [http://www.cbo.gov/showdoc.cfm?index=3641&sequence=0]. See also House Report 107-609, part 1, pp. 80-81.

[92] See CRS Report RL31513.

[93] AAAS, June 21 (revised July 24), Special Analysis – "Proposed Dept. of Homeland Security," July 24, 2002.

Table 5. Estimated R&D Funding in the Department of Homeland Security (DHS) Proposed in H.R. 5005 (Dollars in Millions)

Agency	Program	Amount of Currently Authorized Funding in H.R. 5005	New Funding Required in H.R. 5005
Dept. of Energy	Includes all programs that would be transferred to the Under Secretary for Science and Technology, such as chemical/biological; parts of non-proliferation and verification R&D; nuclear smuggling; part of international materials protection programs; parts of biological and environmental research; advanced scientific computing from Lawrence Livermore Lab; the Environmental Measurements Lab.	$100 (est. by AAAS)	
Dept. of Energy	National Infrastructure Simulation and Analysis Center (NISAC)	$20 (est. by AAAS)	
Dept. of Defense	Transfers from DOD the Biological Defense Homeland Security Support and Biological Counterterrorism Research Program of the Chemical Biological Defense Program.		$420, requested according to OMB for FY2003 for two programs, including this one. Exact amount for the program was not given.
Dept. of Agriculture[94]	Plum Island Center	$25 (est. by AAAS)	
	Animal and Plant Health Inspection Service R&D	$29 (est. by AAAS)	

[94] For additional details, see: Jean M. Rawson, "Homeland Security Department; U.S. Department of Agriculture Issues," CRS Report RL31466, Sept. 6, 2002.

Agency	Program	Amount of Currently Authorized Funding in H.R. 5005	New Funding Required in H.R. 5005
Dept. of Health and Human Services (DHHS) (Largely, NIH's National Institute of Allergy and Infectious Diseases, NIAID)	Bioterrorism R&D Programs	DHS and DHHS would collaborate in setting DHHS bioterrorism R&D priorities. DHS would not control any DHHS bioterrorism R&D funds. These programs would not be transferred to DHS.	
Dept. of Transportation	Coast Guard R&D	$24 (est. by AAAS)	
Transportation Security Administration	Aviation R&D	$130 (est. by the agency for FY2003)	
Other: The new agency's own R&D analysis and support costs	Under Secretary for Science and Technology and the department's science and technology support apparatus, including coordination groups, advisory panels, analysis and evaluation centers, etc.		All funding is new. The amount is unknown
Other: University R&D Centers			$50 (est. by CBO)
Other: "Net Guard"	To assist recovery of information and communication systems after attack. May not involve R&D		$5 annually according to CBO for a similar proposal in S, 2452
Total Newly Authorized Programs Proposed			Estimated at $200 to $400 annually, averaging $300 according to CBO.
Total Currently Authorized Programs		Could be about $300	
Total: About $500 million to $600 million			

Sources: The CBO reference is: Congressional Budget Office, Cost Estimate on H.R. 5005, Homeland Security Act of 2002, as Ordered Reported by the Select Committee on Homeland Security on July 19, 2002, July 23, 2002; AAAS data is from: AAAS, "House Approves Bill to Create a Dept. of Homeland Security...", Aug. 28, 2002, [http://www.aaas.org/spp/rd/dhs0828.htm.]. The OMB source is *OMB, Annual Report to Congress on Combating Terrorism, June 24, 2002*, p. 27.

Proposed for transfer from the Department of Defense is the Biological Defense Homeland Security Support Program and Biological Counter-Terrorism Research Program. DHS would not have responsibility for most DOD bioterrorism R&D. The Agriculture Department's Plum Island Animal Disease Center (R&D on foreign animal diseases) would be transferred to the new department.

Regarding the Department of Health and Human Services (DHHS), the DHHS Secretary, in collaboration with the DHS Secretary would set priorities for certain DHHS R&D for countermeasures for chemical, biological, radiological and nuclear and other terrorist threats. DHS would not have responsibility for funding and conduct of R&D at DHHS. Projects would be carried out in DHHS's National Institutes of Health (NIH), largely in the National Institute of Allergy and Infectious Diseases (NIAID) and in the Centers for Disease Control and Prevention (CDC).

Under Title III, the DHS Under Secretary for Science and Technology is authorized to establish one or more FFRDCs for independent analysis (Sec. 304), and is required to establish one or more university-based centers for homeland security, that would have to meet 15 specific criteria to be funded (Sec. 307). The Under Secretary for Science and Technology would need to consider geographic distribution in the operation of RDT&E programs so as to "ensure that colleges, universities, private research institutes, and companies (and consortia thereof) from as many areas of the United States as practicable participate" (Sec.307). At the same time, the Under Secretary is specifically directed to use merit review guidelines in awarding funds.

Under Title III, the bill would create a Homeland Security Science and Technology Coordination Council to establish R&D priorities within DHS; a Homeland Security Institute to, among other things, conduct analysis and evaluation of the effectiveness of security measures; a Homeland Security Science and Technology Advisory Committee, composed of external experts, first responders, and other stakeholders; a Technology Clearinghouse to encourage innovative solutions and screen proposals in coordination with TSWG. The Under Secretary for Science and Technology could use the expertise of any federal laboratory and could select a "headquarters" laboratory at any national laboratory, to which other laboratories might be added. The bill would also create a science and technology national "Net Guard," to help information systems recover after attack (sec. 213).

Section 202 specifies that the National Infrastructure Simulation and Analysis Center, (currently run by two DOE national laboratories, Sandia and Los Alamos, with a budget of $20 million for FY2002)[95] would be transferred to the DHS Under Secretary for Information Analysis and Infrastructure Protection created by Title II of the bill. The Border and Transportation Security Division of the proposed DHS would include a small amount of R&D, which, according to AAAS, would include Coast Guard R&D ($24 million in FY2003), the Transportation Security Administration's aviation security R&D (a preliminary estimate of $47 million in FY 2003), and the Agriculture Department's Animal and Plant Health Inspection Service R&D portfolio ($29 million in FY 2003).[96]

The DHS Secretary would have special authority for a period of five years after enactment to waive specific procurement laws in R&D pilot projects (Sec. 731); the ability to implement a set of liability protections for manufacturers of innovative antiterrorism technologies (Sec. 751); and authority over DHHS strategic stockpile functions as defined in P.L. 107-188, the Public Health Security and Bioterrorism Preparedness and Response Act of 2002 (Sec. 905). The bill would add homeland security to the list of topics on which the Director of the Office of Science and Technology Policy is to advise the President, and the OSTP Director is mandated to "work in close consultation and cooperation" with the Office of Homeland Security (Sec. 909).

S. 2452, "National Homeland Security and Combating Terrorism Act"

A cabinet-level Department of National Homeland Security (DNHS), including a Directorate of Science and Technology was proposed in S. 2452 (Lieberman), which had been reported favorably in May, 2002. A substitute bill was filed and agreed to on July 25, 2002 by the Committee on Governmental Affairs.[97] The bill would create a National Office of Combating Terrorism in the White House and a DNHS headed by a Secretary with five directorates, each headed by an Under Secretary. They would deal with Border and Transportation Protection; Intelligence; Critical

[95] AAAS, June 21, 2002.

[96] AAAS, June 21, 2002. See also: AAU, *CFR Weekly Wrapup,* June 7, 2002, and John T. Softcheck, "Homeland Security Department Would Contract for Federal Bioterrorism Research," *Washington Fax,* June 10, 2002.

[97] Subsequently, an amendment (no. 4417) to the substitute bill was filed; the provisions discussed in this report relating to science and technology are not markedly different from those in the two versions. The House counterpart to the original version of S. 2452 was H.R. 4660, a successor to H.R. 1158.

Infrastructure Protection; Emergency Preparedness and Response; Science and Technology and Immigration Affairs. The Under Secretary for Science and Technology created by the bill (Sec. 135) would have somewhat broader responsibilities than in H.R. 5005 to support and conduct R&D; to establish a science and technology strategy for countermeasures R&D; to coordinate with other agencies, including OSTP; and to develop "technology roadmaps" to achieve goals. The new DNHS would also set priorities for, and manage in collaboration with DHHS, certain DHHS bioterrorism countermeasures R&D under joint agreements between DNHS and DHHS.

To be transferred to the DNHS from DOE and its laboratories are the following R&D activities: chemical and biological national security and programs and activities supporting domestic response of the non proliferation and verification R&D program; nuclear smuggling programs related to homeland security within the proliferation detection program of the nonproliferation and verification R&D program, "except that the programs and activities described in this clause may be designated by the President either for transfer to the Department or for joint operation by the Secretary and the Secretary of Energy;" nuclear assessment program and activities of the assessment, detection cooperation program of the international materials protection and cooperation program; and the Environmental Measurements Laboratory. These functions would be managed by an Office of Laboratory Research, which would also administer any funds transferred from DNHS to DHHS for R&D. The Office of Laboratory Research would also establish and direct new R&D facilities, include a science advisor to the Under Secretary and support staff to deal with research priorities related to biological and chemical weapons, the development of drugs, devices, and biologies; and R&D on biological and chemical threat agents. The Lieberman substitute would not transfer programs from Lawrence Livermore National Laboratory to the new Department of Homeland Security. Instead, it would create an Office for National Laboratories, responsible for coordinating and utilizing Department of Energy facilities "to create a networked laboratory system" to support the DNHS's missions.

It is estimated that the DNHS proposed in the bill would have responsibility for R&D funding totaling somewhere between $600 million and $650 million, including $125 million worth of DHHS programs, but exclusive of other existing DHHS programs over which the new department may have some authority. See Table 6.

S. 2452 would create a Science and Technology Council, composed of federal agency officials, to set R&D priorities and coordinate government programs. The Under Secretary would have authority to carry out RDT&E and some prototype projects; DOE's national laboratories could be used to support departmental missions. An "Acceleration Fund for Research and Development of Homeland Security Technologies," to support the external R&D, would be authorized at $200 million for FY2003, using interagency groups to establish its priorities. The bill would establish a Homeland Security Science and Technology Council, under the NSTC to assist with interagency coordination. To encourage technology development and deployment, the bill would create a Security Advanced Research Projects Agency (SARPA), an Office on Risk Analysis and Assessment, an Office of Technology Evaluation and Transition, which would operate in an interagency manner modeled on the TSWG.

Table 6. Estimated R&D Funding in the Department of National Homeland Security (DNHS) Proposed in S. 2452 (Lieberman substitute, agreed to by Senate Committee on Governmental Affairs, July 25, 2002) (Dollars in Millions)

Agency	Program	Authorized Funding (FY2002) in S. 2452	New Funding Required for Programs in S. 2452
Dept. of Commerce	NIST's Computer Security Division	$10.2 (est. by NIST in an interview)	
Dept. of Energy	Includes all programs that are transferred to the Under Secretary for Science and Technology, such as chemical/biological; parts of non-proliferation and verification R&D; nuclear smuggling; part of international materials protection programs; parts of biological and environmental research; advanced scientific computing from Lawrence Livermore Lab; the Environ-mental Measurements Lab.	$100 (est. by AAAS)	
Dept. of Defense	National Bio-Weapons Defense Analysis Center	$420 , estimated by CBO. Established by Sec. 161 of the bill to coordinate public and private research on biological counterterrorism and on area monitoring. Some of this may not be R&D.	
Dept. of Agriculture[98]	Animal and Plant Health Inspection Service R&D	$29 (est. by AAAS)	

[98] For additional details, see: Jean M. Rawson, "Homeland Security Department; U.S. Department of Agriculture Issues," CRS Report RL31466, Sept. 6, 2002.

Agency	Program	Authorized Funding (FY2002) in S. 2452	New Funding Required for Programs in S. 2452
Dept. of Health and Human Services (DHHS) (Largely, NIH's National Institute of Allergy and Infectious Diseases, NIAID)	Bioterrorism R&D Programs	Unknown. DNHS would have final authority for priority-setting for bioterrorism; the relationship to budget control is unclear. DHHS FY2003 bioterrorism funding could be $1.7 billion.	
			$125, est. by CBO for DNHS health research initiatives for civilian bioterrrorism research and new NIH research initiatives.
Dept. of Transportation	Coast Guard R&D	$24 (est. by AAAS)	
Transportation Security Administration	Aviation R&D	$130 (est. for FY2002 by the agency in an interview)	
Other: The new agency's own R&D analysis and support costs	Under Secretary for Science and Technology and the department's science and technology support apparatus, including coordination groups, advisory panels, analysis and evaluation centers, etc.		$20 according to CBO
Other: National Emergency Technology Guard	Database costs and procedures to certify, mobilize and deploy science and technology volunteers.		$5 annually according to CBO

Agency	Program	Authorized Funding (FY2002) in S. 2452	New Funding Required for Programs in S. 2452
Other: Security Advanced Research Projects Agency (SARPA)			$300, and $300 for each of the next 5 years, est. by CBO (this includes $200 for the fund in the next cell, which SARPA would manage)
Other: Acceleration Fund for R&D of Homeland Security Technologies			$200; at least 10% of the funds would be spent on projects with the Coast Guard to protect ports, waterways, and coastal areas, according to CBO.
Total Newly Authorized Programs			Estimated at $350 annually by CBO. Estimates for subsequent years are: FY04, $403 FY05, $456 FY06, $509 FY07, $562
Total Currently Authorized Programs		Unknown, but about $300.	
Total: About $600 million to $650 million for DNHS in S. 2452 (exclusive of non-specified DHHS programs)			

Sources: The CBO reference refers to: Congressional Budget Office, Cost Estimate on H.R. 5005, Homeland Security Act of 2002, as Ordered Reported by the Select Committee on Homeland Security on July 19,2002, July 23, 2002; AAAS data is from: AAAS, "House Approves Bill to Create a Dept. of Homeland Security," Aug. 28,2002, [http://www.aaas.org/spp/rd/dhs0828.htm.]

The Under Secretary of the Directorate of Emergency Preparedness and Response would be given responsibility for "select agent" registration activities (which would affect the conduct of R&D in academic and other nongovernmental laboratories) and for DHHS strategic stockpile functions, both mandated by P.L. 107-188 (Sec. 134). Section 133 of S. 2452 would transfer the R&D-intensive Computer Security Division of NIST to the Directorate of Critical Infrastructure Protection. The inspection service of USDA's Animal, Plant, and Health Inspection Service (APHIS), would be transferred to DNHS, as would the Coast Guard and the Transportation Security Administration (both of which have R&D functions) (Sec. 131). Under section 133, research and analysis units would be established to assess vulnerabilities and protective measures for critical infrastructure, such as energy, transportation, water, and so forth. Some cyber-security and physical security for infrastructure functions would be conducted within the DNHS (sec. 133). Also, the bill would create a National Emergency Technology Guard.

Chapter 7

COUNTERTERRORISM R&D PROCUREMENT, ANALYSIS, OR EVALUATION CENTERS

Proposals have been made to create dedicated Counterterrorism R&D analysis and evaluation centers. These vary, but include such concepts as a RAND-like FFRDC,[99] an enhanced Defense Advanced Research Projects Agency (DARPA) for Counterterrorism R&D which would use DARPA's special R&D procurement procedures to rapidly develop antiterrorism technologies,[100] a new "Manhattan" project,[101] special Counterterrorism forecasting centers for creative R&D,[102] and a homeland security institute with testing capabilities. Both H.R. 5005 and S. 2452 contain proposals to create these kinds of organizations. Among the policy issues likely to be considered in assessing these proposals is the value of continuing, but

---

[99] Joseph S. Nye, "How to Protect the *Homeland,*" *New York Times, Editorial,* Sept. 25, 2001.

[100] DARPA is the central R&D agency for the Defense Dept. It manages and directs selected basic and applied R&D projects and pursues research and technology where risk and payoff are both very high for military missions. DARPA gives its program managers considerable autonomy to select creative university and industrial scientists to conduct problem-solving R&D at the cutting edge without having to adhere to rigorous competitive awards procedures customarily used in awarding federal grants and contracts. See Maxine Singer, "Answers From Outside the Box," *Washington Post,* Sept. 14, 2001, p. A21 and William B. Bonvillian and Kendra V. Sharp, "Homeland Security Technology," *Issues in Science and technology OnLine,* Winter 2001. A proposal for a DARPA-like program at NIH was made in Testimony of Richard Klausner, M.D., Senior Fellow and Special Advisor for Counterterrorism, National Academy of Sciences Before the Committee on Commerce, Science, and Transportation, U.S. Senate, Feb. 5, 2002.

[101] Albert R. Hunt, "An Accelerated Agenda for the Terrorism Threat," *Wall Street Journal,* October 25, 2001, p. A21.

[102] "U.S. Army Seeks Hollywood Theories," *MSNBC News,* Oct. 8, 2001. See also: [http://www.ceto.quantico/usmc.mil/about.asp].

enlarging, the functions of existing units versus establishing new mechanisms dedicated to homeland security.

CREATIVE R&D FUNDING MECHANISMS

Reportedly, the private sector has been actively submitting proposals and ideas for Counterterrorism technology to the government and the government "is being courted with an aggressiveness seldom matched."[103] In addition, DOD has initiated several creative programs to develop Counterterrorism R&D technology.[104] Also, OSTP Director Marburger

---

[103] Ariana Eunjung Cha, "High-Tech Firms Vie to Fight Terrorism, Government Deluged by Security Ideas That Are More Practical Than Innovative," *Washington Post,* Mar. 31, 2002.

[104] The importance of procuring or adapting commercial off-the-shelf technologies for security/defense-related needs was underscored in DOD's *Quadrennial Defense Review Report,* issued on September 30, 2001. (Richard M. Jones, "DOD Report Calls for 3% Investment in *S&T," FYI: The AIP Bulletin of Science Policy News,* No. 130, Oct. 18, 2001. See also Statement of OSTP Director John Marburger at AAAS Symposium on "The War on Terrorism: What Does it Mean for Science?," Dec. 18, 2001 and Jennifer B. Lee, "Federal Agents Look to Adapt Private Technology," *New York Times,* Jan. 14, 2002.) In addition, to TSWG, DOD has initiated several programs to enhance cooperation with industry to obtain R&D and technology to combat terrorism. The DOD FY2002 budget request included a proposal for a Quick Reaction Special projects (QRSP) initiative that was not funded, and funding for it was requested again in the FY2003 budget. The stated objective of the initiative was to give DOD budgetary flexibility to enhance DOD's ability to respond rapidly to urgent needs using technology. (Statement of the Honorable Ronald M. Sega, Director Defense Research and Engineering Before the Senate Armed Services Committee, Apr. 10, 2002.)

In-Q-Tel, a private nonprofit venture capital firm set up and financed by the Central Intelligence Agency in late 1999 has been financing start-up companies in order to obtain new technologies. Since the September terrorist attacks, it, reportedly, has received many calls from innovators and firms seeking to develop counterterrorism technologies. Some believe that DOD should consider a model like this to obtain technology. (Amy Cortese, "Suddenly, Uncle Sam Wants to Bankroll You," *New York Times,* Dec. 30, 2001; Shannon Henry, "In-Q-Tel, Investing in Intrigue; CIA Unit Scours Country for Useful Technologies," *Washington Post,* July 1, 2002, p. E01.) "Recently, the Army began considering the creation of a $50 million venture fund modeled after In-Q-Tel." (Cortese, op. cit.)

The Defense Advanced Research Projects Agency (DARPA) held a conference on "Scientists Helping America," on March 11-13, 2002. It was co-sponsored by the U.S. Special Operations Command ... and brought researchers to come to Washington, D.C. to learn about the technical areas where their help is needed and how to apply for contracts. DOD was particularly interested in researchers who have never worked with DOD, and who might have innovative ideas in nine key technical areas: advanced training systems, batteries and fuel cells, bioengineering and chemical/biological defense, directed energy weapons, wide-bandwidth reach-back communications, remote sensing, signature reduction, underwater communications and unmanned systems. ("DARPA, Special testified in April 2002 that there are technologies or uses that do not fit within the "purview of the TSWG," and "the government is 'still struggling to cope with generic or general proposals that are coming from the private sector for addressing the vulnerabilities of large systems,' such as energy, transportation and the mail, that 'do not generally yield to individual technology support on a small scale.'"[105] On May 22, 2002, he testified before the Senate Commerce, Science and Transportation Committee's Science, Technology and Space Subcommittee, that the Administration was considering expanding the interagency Technical Support Working Group to create an "R&D clearinghouse that would manage proposals for combating terrorism."[106] "The procurement and review process of the Technical Support Working Group... ," he said, "'seem[s] to us to be working quite well....' The ... Administration is considering broadening the mission so the panel would be charged to 'solicit, review and respond to unsolicited ideas across broad categories.'" He added that an expanded TSWG would not obviate the review responsibilities of other existing agencies but "would attempt to eliminate funding duplication between agencies."[107] The "White House." he said, "also is contemplating creating a central web site listing agency information and points of contact relating to technology approaches for security and emergency preparedness and response, as well as solicitations and instructions for submitting ideas to a central R&D clearinghouse."[108]

Operations Command Invite Scientists to Help America," *DARPA News Release*, Jan. 15, 2002.)

Reportedly, since September 11th, DARPA has created an Information Exploration Office, that "... develops technology to identify global targets and monitor them until the weapon arrives; then it takes over control of the weapon. John Poindexter, who was national security adviser under President Reagan, heads the new Information awareness Office, which is developing a technology, called "total information awareness," that will detect, track, and pre-empt attacks by identifying terrorist networks through behavior such as financial transactions. The system prototype is expected to be ready in September." (William New, "White House: Back to the Future," *National Journal*, June 15, 2002.)

105 Lauren Hafner, "S&T Response to Emerging Antiterror Needs Requires Flexibility, Senate Panel Hears," *Washington Fax*, Apr. 11,2002.

106 Lauren Hafner, "Proposed Homeland Security Clearinghouse Would Triage Unsolicited Anti-terrorism Proposals," *Washington Fax*, June 4, 2002.

107 Hafner, June 4, 2002.

108 Hafner, June 4, 2002.

Legislative Proposals

As noted above, H.R. 5005 would create a Technology Clearinghouse to encourage innovative solutions and screen proposals in coordination with TSWG. Similarly, S. 2452 would create an Office of Technology Evaluation and Transition which would operate in an interagency manner modeled on TSWG. At least two other bills address this issue.

S. 2037, "Science and Technology Emergency Mobilization Act"

Provisions to use the TSWG model, including a web site and interagency concept, were included in S. 2037, reported amended on June 27, by the Committee on Commerce, Science, and Transportation. Among other things, the bill would establish a Center for Civilian Homeland Security Technology Evaluation within the executive branch to evaluate innovative technologies relating to security and to serve as a national clearinghouse for such technologies.

H.R. 4629, "To Encourage and Support Innovative Proposals to Enhance Homeland Security"

Introduced on May 1, 2002, and referred to the Committee on Government Reform, this bill would direct the Administrator of the Office of Federal Procurement Policy, located in OMB, to establish a Government-wide program to encourage and recognize contractor innovation and excellence in facilitating the defense of the United States against, or recovery from, terrorism or nuclear, biological, chemical, or radiological attack. It also directs the Administrator to establish a pilot program under which the Secretaries of Defense, Energy, Commerce, Transportation, and the Treasury could streamline acquisition procedures for using commercial, off-the-shelf items.

PROPOSALS FOR A HOMELAND SECURITY INSTITUTE

Proposals to create a homeland security institute have been made by both expert groups and legislators. As discussed above, the President, in his Homeland Security Strategy document, as well as PCAST and the National Academies proposed creating a unit with capability to perform independent homeland security analysis and evaluation functions. The units proposed would be responsible for a variety of functions, including RDT&E, analysis and evaluation of technologies. These and other proposals are discussed next.

National Academies' Proposal

The National Academies concluded that because "technical capabilities to provide the analysis necessary to support" a DHS or OHS "do not currently exist in the government in a united and comprehensive form," a Homeland Security Institute to provide technical analysis and support should be established as a "a dedicated, contracted, not-for-profit organization that would serve the organization [whether a DHS or OHS] that sets priorities for homeland security by performing the following functions":

- Systems analysis, risk analysis, and simulation and modeling to determine the vulnerabilities of the nation's critical infrastructures and the effectiveness of the systems deployed to reduce them.
- Sophisticated economic and policy analysis to assess the distributed costs and benefits of alternative approaches to enhancing security.
- Red teaming to evaluate the effectiveness of measures deployed to enhance the security of target institutions, facilities, and infrastructure.
- Identification of instances when common standards and protocols are necessary to ensure interoperability and effective utilization of tools developed for field operators and first responders. The institute would cooperate with relevant federal agencies, such as NIST, in the development of these standards.
- Assistance for agencies in establishing testbeds to evaluate the effectiveness of technologies under development and to assess the appropriateness of such technologies for deployment.
- Design of metrics and use of these metrics to evaluate the effectiveness of homeland security programs throughout the government agencies and at national laboratories.
- Design of and support for the conduct of exercises and simulations.[109]

[109] *Making the Nation Safer*, pp. 12-7 to 12-8.

H.R. 4029, "National Integrative Center for Homeland Security"

Introduced on March 20, 2002, the bill would require the Director of the Federal Emergency Management Agency (FEMA) to establish and operate a center to provide a coordinated, science-based approach to enhance the nation's homeland security and to "establish a university-affiliated homeland security program that integrates ... information services, research, development, evaluation, education, training, and field delivery of responder services...." The bill was referred to the Committee on Transportation Infrastructure.

Related Proposals in H.R. 5005 and S. 2452

The House-passed bill, H.R. 5005, would create a Homeland Security Institute along the lines of the Academies' proposal. In addition, both H.R. 5005 and S. 2452 would permit a homeland security department to utilize national laboratories for the conduct of RDT&E. H.R. 5005 would permit designation of a headquarters laboratory and use of other national labs. S. 2452 would give the Under Secretary for Science and Technology authority to carry out RDT&E and some prototype projects, as well as to use DOE's national laboratories to support departmental missions. The Senate bill would create an Office for National Laboratories to establish a networked laboratory system to support the DNHS's missions. A proposal to create a DARPA-like Security Advanced Research Projects Agency (SARPA) was included in S. 2452. The Senate bill does not propose creation of a Homeland Security Institute, but it would create an office of Risk Analysis and Assessment, with responsibility to evaluate scientific findings.

PROPOSALS FOR SCIENCE AND TECHNOLOGY RESPONDERS

H.R. 4546, the DOD reauthorization bill for FY2003, which passed the House on May 9, 2002, would create a center for the transfer of military technology to emergency "first responders." (The Senate-passed version does not contain the provision; a conference is underway.) It would make available to domestic first responders cutting-edge technology that the federal government has funded for the military. The center would be run by a nonprofit entity that can transfer defense technologies. H.R. 5005 would create a science and technology national "Net Guard," to help information systems recover after attack. S. 2452 would create a National Emergency Technology Guard with broader areas of application.

Chapter 8

OPTIONS TO MODIFY FEDERAL ORGANIZATION FOR INTERAGENCY PRIORITY-SETTING AND COORDINATION

Debates continue about the most effective and efficient way to set priorities and to fund and manage counterterrorism R&D that is now conducted separately in different federal agencies and that is coordinated through mechanisms attached to the Executive Office of the President or other mechanisms for specific R&D areas. This is a complex problem because policy decisions need to conform with the requisites of both security and the conduct of science. Homeland security requirements help define the R&D areas which necessitate coordinated governmental action. Given the character of today's terrorist threats, these involve a vast and diverse range of issues involving virtually every scientific and technical discipline and application, such as communications, health, and transportation. At the same time, the conduct of effective R&D compels attention to the need to balance long-range and more short-term, applied research; and to develop and test, and then to procure and deploy, efficient and effective technological responses. Questions have been raised about whether there are gaps in coverage of some areas and the potential for wasteful duplication of resources in other areas as more funds are made available for counterterrorism R&D and agencies vie to share these resources. There are also issues about which counterterrorism R&D functions should be combined in a homeland security department and which others should be coordinated at the interagency level through the OSTP, NSTC, and OHS, or by a proposed Under Secretary for Science and Technology in a new department, even if those R&D functions continue to be supported and conducted by existing federal agencies.

Coordination By Offices in the Executive Office of the President: Policy Issues

OSTP and OHS in the Executive Office of the President (EOP) have principal responsibility for coordination of counterterrorism R&D. The Technical Support Working Group, led by Departments of State and of Defense, and comprised of most other federal agencies as members, also coordinates funding and development of some antiterrorism technologies and equipment of use to more than one agency. These arrangements were summarized above in Tables 3 and 4.

There are several *advantages* to coordinating counterterrorism R&D priority-setting and collaboration through offices in the EOP. These offices can marshal agency personnel effectively and quickly to develop policies and discuss priorities in rapidly changing areas since a coordination apparatus already exists. Also, these bodies advise the President on policy and are composed largely of senior-level agency and cabinet officials who have authority to set and enforce policies. The major *disadvantage* is that these offices and groups do not have budgetary authority over any programs or agencies.

In order to achieve better coordination at this level, the National Academies stressed that "OMB should prepare and issue jointly with OSTP an annual budget crosscut describing how the present and proposed budgets reflect the S&T priorities for countering terrorism. A joint letter would be transmitted to Congress, with the budget proposed the following January."[110] Also, OMB, according to the National Academies, should improve its definitions and data collection about counterterrorism R&D in collaboration with the OSTP. Regarding *OMB's Annual Report to Congress on Combating Terrorism,* it concluded that:

> ... [T]he definition of "research," and assurance of its consistent interpretation across the agencies, need more work. Categories like "critical infrastructure protection" are not distinct from "counterterrorism," so that the funding representation is not unique. Further refinement of the

[110] *Making the Nation Safer,* pp. 12-9 to 12-10.

> budgeting process at all stages, together with tighter coordination within the EOP, will help assure the coherence of agency programs and their conformity with Presidential priorities. OMB must also work with and support OSTP in coordinating agency activities and offering budget guidance. [It recommended that]... OMB's Annual Report to Congress on Combating Terrorism should include a description of progress toward achieving the goals of the S&T agenda for countering terrorism as well as actual budget appropriations in suitable activity categories and by agency.[111]

OSTP and NSTC have a history of effective coordination in some functional R&D program areas (especially for interagency programs that have been designated as presidential initiatives or for which Congress enacted legislation mandating R&D coordination, notably global climate change and information technology development). Thus, it is possible that NSTC's antiterrorism task force working groups could play an effective role in coordinating programs if the President emphasized using them. OSTP also has well-established relationships with other federal agencies, the scientific community, academia, and the National Academies. It has a nongovernmental advisory body, PCAST, and its own FFRDC to conduct policy analyses. However, since President Bush did not name his OSTP Director as science advisor and the OSTP Director is not a member of several core bodies in the OHS, the OSTP Director may not have authority needed to convince other agencies to take action relating to counterterrorism R&D.

There is little information about the role played in coordinating homeland security R&D by the Homeland Security Council's Policy Coordinating Committee on R&D (HSC's PCC on R&D). Coordination by an OHS group like this offers the advantage of linking R&D priorities directly to intelligence about threats and also to the President's policies to deal with terrorism. OSTP is a member of this PCC. Linkages between the PCC on R&D and the NSTC's antiterrorism working groups have not been described. These two groups could continue to provide a basis for interagency R&D coordination even if a homeland security department were created since neither proposed department, that is DHS nor DNHS, would have the neutral and centralized R&D coordination authority that extends throughout the government, as the PCC on R&D does.

Both H.R. 5005 and S. 2452 propose mechanisms for coordinating R&D. The Under Secretary for Science and Technology in each bill has

---

[111] *Making the Nation Safer,* pp. 12-9 to 12-10.

responsibility for coordinating R&D for units within the department. However, the coordination mechanism proposed in S. 2452 (the Science and Technology Council and the Homeland Security Science and Technology Council) seems to have wider authority to coordinate and interact with R&D programs and agencies outside of the proposed department. In H.R. 5005, the responsibilities of the proposed coordination mechanism (the Homeland Security Science and Technology Coordination Council) are more limited to coordinating R&D within the proposed DHS.

H.R. 5005 contains provisions which appear to maintain the OHS and which link formally OSTP and OHS. The Senate bill, S. 2452, does not mention OHS and creates instead a statutorily authorized Office of Combating Terrorism in the White House which is to work cooperatively with the OSTP Director and the DNHS Secretary and others in developing strategies and programs. OSTP has a wider role in the coordination, strategy, priority-setting and budgetary mechanisms established in S. 2452 than in H.R. 5005. It remains to be determined what span of authority a final version of a department of homeland security would have to monitor and coordinate counterterrorism R&D for programs remaining outside of the department and for which it would have no budgetary authority and what kind of links should there be between a homeland security department and existing interagency coordination mechanisms. This question may be important because other agencies might perceive the proposed new department's R&D priority-setting and coordination activities being biased by the self-interest of its mission.

Interagency Coordination for Bioterrorism R&D

It should also be noted that separate priority-setting and coordination mechanisms have been established for bioterrorism R&D and for information security R&D.

For FY 2003, R&D spending for defense against bioterrorism was requested at $2.435 billion, an almost 5-fold increase over FY2002. Both agencies with major roles in this area, DOD and DHHS, have identified detailed priorities for FY2003. (See Appendix 2 for detailed information about federal agency bioterrorism R&D programs and coordination.)

Formal bioterrorism R&D coordination mechanisms have been developed within and between DOD and DHHS, probably because of the importance of bioterrorism R&D, the amount of resources being devoted to it. DHHS and DOD sponsor the bulk of federal bioterrorism R&D. See Table 7. In addition, Section 108 of P.L, 107-188, the Public Health Security and Bioterrorism Preparedness and Response Act of 2002, created an "Interdepartmental Working Group on Bioterrorism and Other Public Health Emergencies," chaired by the Secretary of DHHS and composed of major federal agency heads, to recommend policies relating to the prevention, preparedness, and response to bioterrorism and other public health emergencies. Section 102 of P.L. 107-188 gave a statutory basis to the position of Assistant Secretary of Public Health Emergency Preparedness that the DHHS Secretary has created previously. Other coordination mechanisms within the EOP that have tangential responsibilities for coordinating bioterrrorism R&D include OSTP's Interagency Microbe Project Working Group and the Homeland Security Council's Policy Coordination Committees that deal with Research and Development and with Medical and Public Health Preparedness. Some aspects of bioterrorism R&D are also being coordinated in NSTC via the "Biological and Chemical Preparedness Working Group." Since S. 2452 (the Lieberman substitute under consideration) gives more authority to the DNHS Secretary than to the DHHS Secretary to set bioterrorism R&D priorities, the responsibilities of existing coordination groups could become secondary to the role of the new Secretary if S.2452 were enacted. Under H.R. 5005, the DHHS Secretary is to collaborate with the DHS Secretary in setting bioterrorism R&D priorities. As a result, the interagency coordinating devices might retain more authority if this bill were adopted.

Information Security R&D Coordination

(See Appendix 3 for a comprehensive discussion.) Details about federal funding for counterterrorism-related information security R&D are unclear. It has been estimated that at least S243 million may be allocated to this field for FY2003.[112] The coordination of information security R&D has been formalized, pursuant to Executive Order 13231, October 16, 2001,[113] within the office of the Special Advisor to the President for Cyber Space Security and the President's Critical Infrastructure Protection Board. These units have general responsibility for information security infrastructure and authority to require agencies to allocate budgetary resources to priority R&D topics that

112 See Appendix Table 2.

113 Executive Order 13231, "Critical Infrastructure Protection in the Information Age," Oct. 16, 2001, 66 FR 53063 to 66 FR53071.

serve the board's agenda. These activities are coordinated with the National Security Council, OHS, OSTP, DARPA and NSF. See Table 8. The need to collaborate closely with industry in information security R&D and other aspects of infrastructure protection may have motivated creation of a separate interagency coordination mechanism. There are indications that this mechanism has identified R&D priorities and may have compelled agencies to allocate budgetary resources for projects to meet the board's requirements. The NSTC working group on "Protection of Vulnerable Systems" may engage in R&D priority-setting and coordination for information security R&D.

Table 7. Organization for Interagency Coordination of Bioterrorism R&D

Office of Science and Technology Policy (OSTP)
Interagency Microbial Project Working Group
National Science and Technology Council (NSTC)
Biological and Chemical Preparedness Working Group (DOD, HHS, CIA, DOC, DOE, DOT, EPA, NSF, USDA, DOT/FBI, VA, STATE, DOI, NASA, Treasury, OMB, NSC, OHS, OSTP)
Department of Health and Human Services (DHHS)
Interdepartmental Group on Bioterrrorism and Other Public Health Emergencies (HHS, USDA, CIA, DOD, DOE, Labor, VA, (P.L. 107-188)
Assistant Secretary of Public Health Emergency Preparedness (P.L. 107-188)
Department of Defense (DOD)
Joint Service Chemical and Biological Defense Program, chaired by Assistant Secretary for Chemical and Biological Defense, pursuant to P.L. 103-160

Source: Prepared by CRS.

There are no provisions in H.R. 5005 relating to information security R&D. S. 2452 would transfer NIST's Computer Security Division, which conducts R&D, to the Critical Infrastructure Protection Division (sec. 133) and would give the Under Secretary for Critical Infrastructure Protection some responsibilities for cyber-security. The proposed DNHS is not given a major role in information security R&D priority setting and cooperative activities. As a result, the interagency coordination apparatus established last fall by the President for information security R&D could continue to play an important role if a homeland security department were created.

Table 8. Existing Mechanisms for Interagency Coordination of Information Security R&D

Executive Office of the President (EOP)
– Special Advisor and Presidential Assistant for Cyber Space Security, Richard Clarke
– *Office of Science and Technology Policy (OSTP)*
– The OSTP Director was named as a member of the interagency President's Critical infrastructure Protection Board, which is to coordinate with the OSTP Director to develop a federal R&D program for information systems (E.0.13231)
National Science and Technology Council (NSTC)
– Interagency Working Group on Critical Infrastructure Protection for Research and Development
– Interagency Working Group on Information Technology Research and Development, which has a Committee on Technology which also supports the President's Information Technology Advisory Committee (P.L. 102-194)
– Protection of Vulnerable Systems Work Group, which has an R&D Working Group jointly headed by the OSTP Director and the Special Advisor for Cyber Space Security
Office of Homeland Security (OHS)
– President's Critical Infrastructure Protection Board Chaired by Special Advisor to the President for Cyber Space Security, who reports both to the Presidential Assistant for National Security and the Assistant for Homeland Security. The OSTP Director is a member of the board, which has a R&D Subcommittee chaired by the OSTP director (E.0.13231)

Source: Prepared by CRS.

R&D in a Homeland Security Department: Policy Issues

The span of responsibility for counterterrorism R&D is more limited in the DHS created by H.R. 5005 than in the DNHS created in the substitute version of S. 2452. The homeland security department proposed in the House-passed bill could have responsibility for about $500 to $600 million worth of counterterrorism R&D in total. The CBO estimated that annual funding for newly authorized R&D in H.R. 5005 would tally about $300 million. This is in addition to the funds for R&D which are already authorized for programs to be transferred to DHS, estimated between $200 million to $300 million. Newly authorized R&D that would be handled by the department created in the S. 2452 would total at least $350 million, with funding for already authorized programs totaling an additional $200 to $300 million, for a total approaching $650 million. Each bill would create an agency with R&D responsibilities transferred from DOE, DOD, the Coast Guard, the Agriculture Department, and the Transportation Security Administration. DNHS would have more responsibly for R&D than DHS since it would also manage the Computer Security Division proposed to be transferred from NIST in the Commerce Department, a $200 million R&D fund to be managed by the proposed SARPA, and other R&D related responsibilities that are not in DHS. Also, it would have more responsibility than the DHS proposed in H.R. 5005 for setting priorities and funding bioterrorism R&D in DHHS. While the agency created under each bill would have transferred to it some DOD bioterrorism R&D responsibilities, most military-oriented bioterrrorism responsibilities would remain outside of either department, including the U.S. Army Medical Research Institute of Infectious Disease in Fort Detrick MD, the nation's premier biodefense lab. The proposed DNHS would have broader authority than the proposed DHS to work with other agencies to coordinate counterterrorism R&D programs and strategies.

There is continuing concern about the actual content of a proposed homeland security department's span of R&D responsibilities in relation to other federal counterterrorism R&D programs that remain outside of the department. If a homeland security department were responsible for about $500 million worth of R&D, that would constitute about 17% of the FY2003 $3 billion counterterrorism R&D budget. This may mean that a large portion of the counterterrorism R&D budget remaining outside of a new department either is not related to homeland security, or that much homeland security related R&D would not be managed by the homeland security department. In order to resolve these issues, in a July 2002 report, PCAST recommended that OSTP in conjunction with OMB, OHS and DHS should "identify each federal R&D program that has relevance to homeland security." Then the lists could be consolidated and Congress and DHS should be made aware of the lists to help them determine DHS's responsibility for homeland security R&D programs.[114]

---

[114] PCAST, *Report on Maximizing the Contribution of Science and Technology Within the New Department of Homeland Security,* July 23, 2002, op. cit.

Chapter 9

CONCLUDING OBSERVATIONS: ISSUES FOR CONGRESS

This book has summarized current programs and mechanisms for counterterrorism R&D priority-setting and coordination, and has described alternative proposals to create a new homeland security department with R&D responsibilities. Debates about these issues are continuing in Congress. Topics that might warrant congressional attention are identified next.

ARGUMENTS IN FAVOR OF R&D IN A NEW DEPARTMENT

Those favoring creation of a new homeland security department with responsibilities for managing core counterterrorism R&D say such a department could,

- Give considerable visibility to counterterrorism R&D budgets;[115]
- Bring some scientists who do counterterrorism R&D together in one department and increase their influence in national security debates;[116]
- Enhance the contributions of DOE nuclear weapons laboratories, which might offer substantial assets for homeland security, and

[115] Brookings, July 2002, p. 26.
[116] Brookings, July 2002, p. 26.

once good technologies were developed, help to accelerate their deployment more quickly and possibly more economically than DOE or HHS would have been able to do;[117]

- Project clear responsibility and authority for some counterterrorism R&D;
- link priority setting clearly to intelligence information and homeland security threats; and
- Augment current organizational arrangements for counterterrorism R&D by establishing a way to manage and oversee the analysis, evaluation, and testing bodies proposed to be created in order to hasten development and deployment of new counterterrorism technologies.

CONCERNS ABOUT R&D IN A NEW DEPARTMENT

Others caution that important questions need to be answered in designing a new department with R&D responsibilities. These include,

- Is the Administration's homeland security R&D policy sufficiently well-formulated to determine R&D priorities for a homeland security department and to define the rationale and relationships between the R&D that will be consolidated (about 17% of the current federal counterterrorism R&D budget) and the rest of the counterterrorism R&D that will remain outside of DHS?[118]
- Would the department give adequate attention to prevention and R&D priorities that deal with controlling dangerous materials, sensors, surveillance and data management?[119]
- Would attention be given to maintaining dual-use or dual-purpose R&D programs that have both civilian and security applications[120]

---

117 Brookings, July 2002, p. 26.
118 For a general discussion of this topic, see Brookings, July 2002.
119 Brookings, July 2002, pp. vii and 28.
120 Statement of Ms. Gary L. Jones, "Homeland Security, Title III of the Homeland Security Act of 2002," Testimony before the Subcommittee on Oversight and Investigations, Committee on Energy and Commerce, July 9, 2002, pp. 2 and 7.

so that there will be no compromise to the natural synergies and communications between researchers, which is important to scientific advancement and to avoid duplication of effort?[121]

- If a proposed homeland security department were to be given more responsibility for bioterrorism research, what steps should the department take to ensure adequate support for the fundamental research and science needed?[122] How should a new department interface with the existing mechanisms for coordination of counterterrorism R&D in the agencies, the OHS, OSTP, NSTC, statutorily mandated bodies, and other existing interagency mechanisms? What would be the specific lines of communication and responsibility between the directors of OSTP and OHS on the one hand, and the Under Secretary for Science and Technology in a new department on the other?

- Where, in a DHS, in a DNHS, or in existing EOP agencies, should attention be given to research policy issues identified as critical to homeland security R&D, including proposals for enhancing industrial R&D; collecting better information about the funding of federal counterterrorism R&D; balancing the conduct of science

---

[121] On this point a GAO official testified "... [W]e believe that some of the transfers proposed in the legislation are appropriate, such as DOE's nuclear threat assessment program and the Environmental Measurements Laboratory (EML). However, we are concerned that the transfer of certain DOE research and development activities may complicate research currently being performed to accomplish multiple purposes. For example, some research programs, such as Lawrence Livermore National Laboratory's advanced scientific computing research program, have broad missions such as ensuring the reliability of our nuclear weapons stockpile that are not easily separated into homeland security research and research for other purposes." [Regarding proliferation detection research], "These programs have broad missions that are not easily separated into homeland security research and research for other purposes and the proposed legislation is not clear how these missions would continue to be accomplished. Furthermore, we are concerned that the legislation does not clearly indicate whether only the programmatic management and funding would move or also the scientists carrying out the research. Moving the scientists may not be prudent. This is because the research is currently conducted by multi program laboratories that employ scientists skilled in many disciplines who serve many different missions and whose research benefits from their interactions with colleagues within the laboratory" [Perhaps DHS could contract for work to be done by DOE laboratories] (Jones, pp. 8-9).

[122] "Homeland Security: New Department could Improve coordination but May Complicate Priority Setting," Statement of Janet Heinrich, Before the Committee on Governmental affairs, U.S. Senate, June 28, 2002, p.2. See also Brookings, p. vii.

with security sensitive research and information needs;[123] conducting classified research on university campuses; and developing programs to enlarge the number of U.S. students studying science and technology?

- Would creation of a new department necessitate changes to existing multiple congressional committee authorization and appropriations jurisdiction for R&D in order to enhance congressional oversight and appropriations processes for homeland security R&D?[124]

[123] See, for example, *Possible Impacts of Major Counter Terrorism Security Actions on Research, Development, and Higher Education.* By Genevieve J. Knezo, CRS Report, RL31354.

[124] See William C. Boesman, *A Department of Science and Technology: a Recurring Theme,* CRS Report 95-235 SPR, Feb. 3,1995. 6 p.

Chapter 10

APPENDIX 1. NSTC'S ANTITERRORISM TASK FORCE WORKING GROUPS

(This information was provided by OSTP.)

RADIOLOGICAL, NUCLEAR AND CONVENTIONAL (RNC) WORKING GROUP

The group is tasked: to understand the radiological, nuclear, and conventional threat and associated U.S. vulnerabilities; to develop a prioritized set of goals for detecting and responding to that threat; to understand the technical alternatives for detection and response; and to develop a 5 year R&D program aimed at satisfying the performance goals. The near term work program includes: surveying the threats; reviewing current agency requirements for prevention, detection, response, treatment, decontamination, modeling and simulation, and other required activities; assessing likely progress toward meeting those requirements under current R&D programs; and developing guidance for the FY04 budget. *Membership* – CIA, DOT, DOC, EPA, DOD, NSF, DOE, NSC, DOJ, NRC, DOS, OMB.

Biological and Chemical Preparedness Working Group

The Biological and Chemical Preparedness (BCP) Working Group will bring together Federal agencies that fund and oversee BCP research and development (R&D) efforts or that use the results of such activities. BCP for combating terrorist threats to U.S. citizens and residents (human health), and to animal and plant species of economic or cultural importance to the United States will be the overarching goal of the Working Group's efforts. Issues to be addressed by the BCP Working Group include identifying current BCP R&D activities that can inform the Federal antiterrorism agenda (e.g., assessment of existing identification and detection technologies, databases and bioinformatics programs); identification of technological preparations and response options (e.g., vaccines, treatments, neutralization methodologies, automated response planning systems); determining how R&D efforts can be better linked to current "operational" antiterrorism activities; examining the scope of and linkages between current public and private R&D agendas; assessing the research infrastructure (e.g., capacity, core competency, sources of current expertise); and identifying priorities for strengthening antiterrorism programs. The Working Group will work actively with appropriate groups chartered by the OHS and NSC, and with the National Academies of Science and professional organizations to coordinate efforts and to enlist the participation of appropriate National experts. *Membership* – DOD, HHS, CIA, DOC, DOE, DOT, EPA, NSF, USDA, DOT/FBI, VA, STATE, DOI, NASA, Treasury, OMB, NSC, OHS, OSTP.

Rapid Response Working Group

The Rapid Response Team consists of greater than 25 Federal agencies with expertise and technologies related to homeland security. From the agency points of contact list, small working groups are established on an ad hoc basis to fulfill the mission of the response team working group. The mission is to form expert subgroups in response to timely, emergent issues which require the scientific and technical expertise of the Federal government's agencies. The agency points of contact have the authority to request their agency personnel for aid in rapidly responding to questions, proposals or directives from the Director of OSTP and other White House Offices. The subgroups, through the OSTP representative, will report their findings/ recommendations to the Director of OSTP for the appropriate action. For example, the OSTP Irradiation Technical Team elicited help from the AFRRI/DOD, NIST, USDA, FDA, and DOE to address through experimental design and make recommendations to the USPS on the sterilization of the mail contaminated with Bacillus anthracis. The team continues to function in scientific evaluation of the mail irradiation issue and in ongoing experiments related to the use of X-rays in decontaminating larger packages. Likewise, the OSTP Ethylene Oxide (EtO) Technical Team was assembled with scientific experts from DOJ, EPA, FDA, CDC, CIA, AFRRI/DOD, and OSHA in order to determine the technical parameters and standards of EtO sterilization for decontaminating mail packages and items of the biopathogen. *Membership* – AFRRI, CDC, CIA, DARPA, DOD, DOEd, DOE, DOI, DOJ, DOT, EPA, FBI, FDA, FEMA, HHS, NASA, NOAA, NIC, NIOSH, NIST, NRC, NSF, OHS, OMB, OSHA, State, USDA, USPS, USSS, VA.

Social, Behavioral and Education Sciences (SBE) Working Group[125]

The Social, Behavioral and Education Sciences (SBE) Working group will bring together agencies who oversee SBE R&D efforts that are relevant to antiterrorism activities, as well as agencies with programmatic activities related to the agenda of the working group. Issues to be addressed by the SBE working group include identifying current SBE R&D activities that can inform the federal antiterrorism agenda (e.g., terror management, decision-making analysis, crisis intervention care, etc.), determining how such efforts can be better linked to current antiterrorism planning and response activities, and drafting a coordinated and integrated interagency SBE antiterrorism R&D agenda and budget. The Working Group will actively work with the National Academies of Science and SBE professional organizations to coordinate efforts and to enlist the participation of academic researchers and policy analysts. The group will produce a prioritized portfolio review and recommendations for areas requiring additional R&D funding. *Membership*

[125] Remarks of Dr. John Marburger, OSTP Director, by M.R.C. Greenwood, former Associate Director for Science, OSTP, and Dr. Lewis Branscomb, co-chair of the NAS Committee on Responses to Terrorism, at AAAS R&D Colloquium, Apr. 11, 2002. See : *COSSA Washington Update,* Apr. 15, 2002.

– OSTP, NSF, NIH, DOD, DHHS, VA, NIJ, CDC, OHSA, and ED, with new members being added from the CIA, EPA, NIOSH, DARPA and FBI.

Chapter 11

APPENDIX 2. PRIORITIES, FUNDING, AND COORDINATION OF BIOTERRORISM R&D

FY2003 BIOTERRORISM R&D FUNDING AND PRIORITIES

The President's report, *Securing the Homeland, Strengthening the Nation,* 2002, presented data on cross-agency R&D funding for defending against bioterrorism R&D for FY2003 at $2.435 billion, an almost 5-fold increase over FY2002.[126] See Appendix Table 1.

In a report released in July 2002, the Defense Science Board (DSB) task force report recommended that DOD should "quadruple its annual investment in biowarfare defense from $250 million to $1 billion…."[127] The National Academies' report, *Making the Nation Safer: The Role of Science and Technology in Countering Terrorism,* recommended priorities for bioterrorism R&D,[128] including: new tools for the surveillance, detection and diagnosis of bioterrorist threat agents, "increased knowledge of the pathogenesis of and immune responses to biological infectious agents," the development of new drugs, vaccines and devices to address bioterrorist threats, decontamination and bioterrorism forensics. Two recommendations

---

126 See CRS Report RL31202, pp. 24-26 for activities before Jan. 2002. Total funding for FY2002 was $1.408 billion, for FY2002 supplemental $3,730 billion, and for FY2003 proposed $5,898 billion.

127 John T. Softcheck, "Defense Science Board Task Force Calls for Integrated Biowarfare Defense Initiative," *Washington Fax,* July 24, 2002.

128 See chapter 3.

were categorized as "Urgent Research Opportunities." They were to "develop effective treatments and preventatives for known pathogens for which current responses are unavailable and for potential emerging pathogens," and to "develop new methods and standards for filtering air against both chemicals and pathogens as well as better methods and standards for decontamination."[129]

Appendix Table 1. R&D Funding for Defense against Biological Terrorism (Dollars in millions)

R&D Program	FY2002 Enacted (Base)	FY2002 Supp.	FY2003 Proposed
Basic and applied biodefense research (NIH)	$93	$85	$1,080
Biodefense research infrastructure (NIH)	0	70	336
Anthrax vaccine development (NIH and CDC)	18	0	268
Expedited drug approval/research (FDA)	7	41	49
Research facility security upgrades (HHS)	0	84	100
Bio weapons defense/counter-measures (DOD)			120
Agent identification, detection and area monitoring (DOD)			300
Other R&D (DOD)	182	1	182
Total	**$300**	**$281**	**$2,435**

Source: *Securing the Homeland and Strengthening the Budget.* February, 2002 (www.whitehouse.gov/homeland/0 homeland_security_book.pdf).

FY2003 DOD Bioterrorism R&D Priorities

Among the Administration's FY2003 budget initiatives for DOD was a Biological Counterterrorism Research Program which would establish a biological terrorism threat assessment research Center for Biological Counterterrorism at the U.S. Army Medical Research and Materiel Command at Fort Detrick, Maryland. The concepts and scope of research will be developed by "a panel of senior scientists from DOD, federal laboratories, [and the] academic, industry and intelligence communities...."[130] The DOD program would award funds to achieve the following program objectives:

---

[129] P. Es-3.

[130] Klein, Apr. 10, 2002, p. 4.

Biological Counterterrorism Research Program

- Conduct a technology survey and identify gaps.
- Award extramural research with emphasis on identification of virulence factors, pathogenic mechanisms and structural biology.
- Establish research programs in aerobiological research, forensic genomics and certified forensic biological threat agent capability.
- Initiate planning and concept development for necessary infrastructure.
- Develop "Applied Microbial Threat Assessment Research" to assist in the development of the Counterterrorism research program and to establish a management element for the program; develop program policy, strategic plan, short through far term investment strategies.
- Develop environmental and access control point monitoring.
- Develop enhanced medical surveillance technologies.
- Demonstrate an enhanced signatures database and conduct baseline studies.
- Develop improved biological defense data mining, fusion, and analysis architectures.
- Conduct Baseline Self Assessment (BSA), Mission Area Assessments (MAAs), and Requirements Analysis and Process Development.[131]

DOD has also established specific R&D initiatives for monitoring in an urban environment, and for increasing chemical and biological defense capabilities at DOD installations.[132] DOD also supports a Joint Medical Chemical and Biological Defense Research Program. In addition there is a Biological Warfare Defense Program in DARPA.[133] This program was described in hearings held in April 2002 before the Senate Committee on Armed Services. It focuses on "sensors to detect biological agents, vaccines to prevent infection, therapies to treat people who have been exposed, and decontamination technologies…."[134] New initiatives include an unconventional pathogen countermeasures program, biological sensor

[131] Klein, Apr. 10, 2002, p. 4.

[132] Klein, Apr. 10, 2002, pp. 5-6.

[133] Klein, p. 7.

[134] Statement by Dr. Tony Tether, Director, DARPA, Submitted to the Subcommittee on Emerging Threats and Capabilities of the Senate Committee on Armed Services, Apr. 10, 2002.

programs, the "Continuous Assisted Performance Program," to prevent fatigue, and a "Brain Machine Interface Program."[135]

FY2003 DHHS Bioterrorism R&D Priorities

The National Institute of Allergy and Infectious Diseases' (NIAID) FY2003 budget request of $1.7 billion for bioterrorism-related R&D and infrastructure was about a fivefold increase over FY2002. This included about $441 million for basic research, about $592 million for therapeutics, drugs, and vaccines, about $195 million for clinical research and pilot studies for diagnostics involving new vaccines and drugs and about $521 million for facilities and training, including construction and renovation of buildings and facilities, "including establishing a series of extramural and intramural Centers of Excellence for bioterrorism and Emerging Infections" with higher biosafety levels for research laboratories.[136] NIATD's plans for research to protect against bioterrorism agents such as smallpox, anthrax, tularemia, and plague, viral hemorrhagic fevers, and botulism, were identified in its report, *NIAID Counter-Bioterrorism Research Agenda for CDC Category A Agents* and in its broad strategic for research on potential bioterrorism pathogens, Strategic Plan for Counter-Bioterrorism Research of the NIAID.[137]

BIOTERRORISM R&D COORDINATION MECHANISMS IN DOD AND DHHS

DOD's coordination mechanisms were created before the September 11th attacks. In 1993, Congress passed P.L. 103-160, of which Section 1703 created a Joint Service Chemical and Biological Defense Program (JSCBDP), with responsibility to develop and oversee the defense chemical and biological R&D program. It is chaired by a Deputy Assistant to the Secretary of Defense for Chemical and Biological Defense. The JSCBDP

---

135 Tether, Apr. 10, 2002.

136 Ted Agres, "Bioterrorism Projects Boost US Research Budget," *The Scientist,* Mar. 18, 2002. The information came from Anthony Fauci, NIAID Director.

137 Available at [www.niaid.nih.gov/dmid/pdf/bioresearchagenda.pdf.] See also John T. Softcheck, "NIAID Creates Bioterrorism Initiatives to Facilitate Outpouring of Science-Community Support," *Washington Fax,* Dec. 13, 2001.)

establishes priorities, monitors work, and sees that results are integrated into defense programs. It coordinates via informal consultations with other agencies that support or conduct bioterrorism R&D, such as NIH and DOE, to ensure eliminating duplication. It also established and chairs a federal interagency advisory group to deal with the issue of establishing a production facility for "biological defense vaccines." Other participants are from OSTP, the Office of an Homeland Security, the National Security Council, OMB, Federal Emergency Management Agency (FEMA), DHHS agencies.[138] The JSCBDP is required to report to Congress annually.[139]

In June 2001, Dr. Scott Lillibridge, a leading national bioterrorism expert, was named the DHHS Secretary's Special Assistant for National Security and Bioterrorism.[140] On November 1, 2001, to help coordinate the internal response to bioterrorism and also to coordinate with other departments, agencies and offices and state and local entities, DHHS Secretary Tommy Thompson created an Office of Public Health Emergency Preparedness, headed by an assistant Secretary, Donald A. Henderson, former director of the Johns Hopkins Center for Civilian Biodefense Studies and one of the nation's leading bioterrorism experts.[141] On May 3, 2002, Jerome Hauer, who has extensive experience in developing bioterrorism response plans and preparedness, was appointed to replace Dr. Henderson, who resigned but continues "to serve as Principal Science Advisor to Secretary Thompson on issues of public health preparedness and chairman of the Council on Public Health Preparedness."[142] The position of Assistant Secretary of Public Health Emergency Preparedness was statutorily created in the Public Health Security and Bioterrorism Response Act of 2002 (Section 102 of P.L. 107-188). It has not been filled, as of September 11, 2002.

---

[138] Statement of Dr. Anna Johnson-Winegar, Deputy Assistant to the Secretary of Defense for Chemical and Biological Defense on Biological Terrorism, before the Senate Committee on Government Affairs, Oct. 17, 2001.

[139] *Department of Defense Chemical and Biological Defense Program, Annual Report to Congress And Performance Plan,* July 2001, pp. 14-15, [http://www.acq.osd.mil/cp/nbc01.pdf]. See *also, Joint Program Chemical and Biological Defense Program Overview, FY2001,* [http://www.acq.osd.mil/cp/reports.html]

[140] "Secretary Thompson Testifies on HHS Readiness and Role of Vaccine Research and Development Tuesday," DHHS Press Office, Oct. 23, 2001.

[141] Ceci Connolly, "U.S. Reorganizes Bioterror Strategy, Moves Aimed at Improving Relations between HHS, CDC," *MSNBC News,* Nov. 8, 2001.

[142] Nura Shehzad, "Hauer to Replace D.A. Henderson as Had of Office of Public Health Preparedness," *Washington Fax,* May 7, 2002.

INTERAGENCY COORDINATION FOR BIOTERRORISM R&D

Informal mechanisms for multi-agency collaboration in bioterrorism R&D involve CDC, FDA, NIH, especially the National Institute of Allergy and Infectious Diseases, and DOD, especially the Army Medical Research Institute of Infectious Diseases (USAMRIID), the Office of Naval Research, and DARPA.[143] Formal interagency coordination takes several forms in addition to the mechanisms already described. Priority-setting and collaboration in genetic sequencing of microbes with possible terrorist implications is being coordinated through OSTP's Interagency Microbe Project Working Group.[144] As noted above, the Homeland Security Council has Policy Coordination Committees to ensure interagency coordination of specific aspects of homeland security. One committee deals with Research and Development and another focuses on Medical and Public Health Preparedness. The secretaries of major departments, including DHHS and DOD, are members of the council and groups which comprise the Homeland Security Agency. There is also a NSTC "Biological and Chemical Preparedness Working Group." In addition, Section 108 of P.L. 107-188 created an "Interdepartmental Working Group on Bioterrorism and Other Public Health Emergencies," chaired by the DHHS Secretary, and composed of the Secretaries of Agriculture, DOD, Energy, Labor, Veterans Affairs, the Attorney General, the Director of Central Intelligence, the Administrator of the Environmental Protection Agency, the Director of the Federal Emergency Management Agency, and other federal officials as appropriate, to recommend policies relating to the prevention, preparedness, and response to bioterrorism and other public health emergencies. Among its responsibilities is "research on pathogens likely to be used in a biological threat or attack on the civilian population."

---

[143] Tommy G. Thompson, "Civilian Preparedness for Biological Warfare and Terrorism: HHS Readiness and Role in Vaccine Research and Development," Testimony Before the Committee on Government Reform, Subcommittee on National Security, Veterans Affairs and International Relations, Oct. 23, 2001.

[144] Robert E. Waldron, Assistant Deputy Administrator for Nonproliferation Research and Engineering National Nuclear Security Administration, U. S. Department of Energy, Before the Subcommittee on Emerging Threats and Capabilities, Committee on Armed Services, United States Senate, Apr. 10, 2002, p. 3.

CONGRESSIONAL ACTIVITIES AND OPTIONS

Numerous congressional hearings addressing bioterrorism research issues, have been held.[145] Major legislative proposals that address bioterrorism R&D have dealt with such issues as enhancing R&D priority-setting and coordination; improving the organization of research, expanding funding for specific kinds of R&D, including R&D at the Department of Veterans' Affairs; and improving cooperation with pharmaceutical firms.

Pending Legislation on Bioterrorism R&D

The provisions relating to DHHS R&D, including bioterrorism prevention activities in H.R. 5005 and S. 2452 were discussed above. Other legislation includes:

S. 2487, "Global Pathogen Surveillance Act." Agreed to in the Senate on August 1, 2002, it would improve the capacity of laboratories in developing countries and their capability to do epidemiological surveillance, by establishing cooperative relationships between United States public health laboratories and foreign counterparts, and by expanding the training and outreach activities of the Centers for Disease Control and Prevention and Department of Defense to enhance the public health capabilities of developing countries. The bill was reported from the Committee on Foreign Relations on May 23, 2002, (Sen. Kept. 107-210).

H.R. 3253, "National Medical Emergency Preparedness Act." Amended and passed in the House on May 20, 2002, (House Report 107-471), and in the Senate on August 1, 2002; conference action completed September 17, 2002. It would establish a four new National Medical Preparedness Centers for R&D on radiological, chemical, and biological threats. R&D and training would be conducted by the Department of Veterans Affairs in cooperation with such other agencies as, NIH, CDC, DOD and the Office of Homeland Security. In addition, the centers would provide laboratory assistance to facilities at state and local levels, during

[145] For a partial list of hearings held in the 107th Congress, see Appendix C in C. Stephen Redhead, Donna U. Vogt, and Mary E. Tiemann, *Public Health Security and Bioterrorism Preparedness and Response Act (P.L. 107-188): Provisions and Changes to Preexisting Law.* CRS Report RL31263, Updated June 25, 2002.

emergencies. $20 million would be authorized for each fiscal year to 2006.

S. 1764, "Robert Stevens, Thomas Morris Jr., Joseph Curseen, Kathy Nguyen, Ottilie Lundgren, and Lisa J. Raines Biological and Chemical Weapons Research Act." Introduced on December 4, 2001, it would provide tax and patent incentives to increase research by commercial entities to develop vaccines, microbicides, diagnostic technologies, and other drugs to prevent and treat illnesses associated with a biological or chemical weapons. It would also authorize the NIH Director to fund the construction of additional biosafety laboratories and "promote joint ventures between the NIH, its grantees, and for-profit biotechnology, pharmaceutical, and medical device industries for the development of countermeasures and research tools." $200 million would be authorized for each of the next five years for the program. No further action has occurred.

S. 2115, "Center for Bioterrorism Preparedness In the Centers for Disease Control and Prevention Research Act." Introduced on April 11, 2002, it would create a Center for Bioterrorism Preparedness and Response within the Centers for Disease Control and Prevention. It would require registration for the possession, use and transfer of biological, chemical and radiological agents and toxins that could threaten public health and safety and development of a list of such agents. No further action has occurred.

CONCLUDING OBSERVATIONS ON COORDINATION OF BIOTERRORISM R&D

It has been recommended that interagency bioterrorism R&D mechanisms be strengthened to inventory R&D funding and programs; set priorities; eliminate duplication; and develop policy for effective collaboration with industry, professional groups, academia and federal laboratories. Steps in this direction are being taken. Existing governmental organization for coordinating bioterrorism R&D is depicted in Table 7. During 2002, Congress mandated a statutorily authorized Assistant Secretary of Public Health Emergency Preparedness and an Interdepartmental Group on Bioterrrorism and Other Public Health Emergencies (P.L. 107-188). That law also set certain priorities for bioterrorism R&D. Legislation is moving through Congress which would give a department of homeland security authority to collaborate with DHHS in setting bioterrorism R&D priorities (H.R. 5005), or to set priorities for DHHS, DOE and other bioterrorism R&D and fund selected DHHS programs with funds transferred from DNHS (S. 2452). These proposals would clearly link DHHS bioterrorism R&D to homeland security intelligence and policy. Other pending legislation would create or augment bioterrorism R&D programs or facilities.

Some critics object to proposals to give a department of homeland security responsibility to set bioterrorism R&D priorities or to challenge the priority decisions made by the DHHS Secretary. They say that the DHHS Secretary is in a better position than the DHS Secretary to set biological sciences R&D priorities, and that progress in countering bioterrorism cannot occur if infectious diseases research is separated from research on toxic agents that could be used by terrorists, such as smallpox.[146] Some say that the DHHS Secretary already is linked to surveillance, research, and treatment functions and this authority is adequate:

> Currently, [DHHS Secretary] Thompson has a one-stop shop at HHS. He has authority over the Public Health Service, which includes the Centers for Disease Control and Prevention (the experts on infectious disease): the Food and Drug Administration (the regulator of vaccines, drugs, and food safety; and the National Institutes of Health (the premier medical research entity.) Moreover HHS is home to the Office of Emergency Preparedness, which seeks to ensure that hospitals and other bioterrorism responders are ready to meet the challenge of an attack. In addition, Thompson has created the Office of Public Health Preparedness to coordinate the department's many efforts on bioterrorism.[147]

An issue that may be considered in assessing whether a homeland department should have more control over bioterrorism R and D is balancing (1) the importance of ensuring a link between homeland security needs as defined by a proposed DHS Secretary using intelligence information and other estimates of vulnerability with (2) the importance of having scientists

---

[146] Jeffrey Brainard, "Scientists Question Plan to Move Bioterrrorism-Research Funds to Homeland-Defense Agency," *Chronicle of Higher Education*, July 5, 2002. Similar views have been expressed by the American Society for Microbiology and the Association of American Universities. Leventhal memo cited in AAU, *CFR Weekly Wrapup*, June 21, 2002.

[147] Marilyn Werber Serafini, "One-stop Shop on Bioterrorism at HHS May Be Split Up," *GovExec.com.*, June 21, 2002.

who work on bioterrorism R&D define priorities based on scientific and technical developments. There is also the need to coordinate all of DOD's extensive bioterrorism R&D activities with those of the new department and DHHS.

Chapter 12

Appendix 3. Information Security R&D

Funding for Information Security R&D

According to the President's Commission on Critical Infrastructure Protection, about $250 million was being invested in FY1997 (the latest year for which R&D data are available) on critical infrastructure protection R&D, with 60%, or $150 million, for information security. The commission recommended an increase ranging from $250 million to $500 million in FY1999, "with incremental increases... over a five-year period to $1 billion in FY04."[148] It is generally acknowledged that DOD provides the lion's share of information security R&D funding because of its mission needs. Precise funding amounts are unknown. However, one of DOD's constituent agencies, the National Security Agency (NSA), reported an information security RDT&E budget of $308 million for FY2000 and requested $415 million for FY2001.[149]

For FY2003, the president's homeland security budget identified as one of four initiatives "Using 21st Century Technology to Defend the Homeland." Total funding requested for IT/information sharing under this category was $722 million. It appears that at least $243 million could be allocated to R&D related to information security. The largest clearly identified R&D funding line was for the NSF program for Research and Physical and Information Technology, at $198 million in FY2002, and

---

[148] *Critical Foundations. Protecting America's Infrastructures. The Report of the President's Commission on Critical Infrastructure Protection,* October 1997, p.89.

[149] DOD, *DOD's Amended FY2001 Budget, R-1* document.

requested at $197 million for FY2003. Elements of information security research were also included in the program initiative, "Cyberspace Security: Protecting Our Information Infrastructure," but the amount for R&D was not separately identified. See Appendix Table 2. These data do not include about $400 million for R&D in the National Security Agency and at the Defense Information Agency, which would appear to support R&D related to information security.[150]

OPTIONS FOR PRIORITY-SETTING

In activities that have occurred since January 2002, a June 2002 National Academies' report recommended cyber-security R&D priorities to protect information systems and develop applications to reduce the nation's vulnerability to terrorist attack.[151] One of the most urgent research needs was to "advance the practical utility of data fusion and data mining for intelligence analysis, and enhance information security against cyberattacks."[152] It also recommended "A strategic long-term research and development agenda should be established to address three primary Counterterrorism-related areas in IT: information and network security, the IT needs of emergency responders, and information fusion."[153]

OPTIONS FOR ORGANIZATION

It is difficult to coordinate R&D for information security R&D. While many federal agencies support relevant R&D, systems applications largely are a private sector responsibility. Suggestions for an organizational format to determine R&D priorities vary from placing the responsibility in a new Office of Homeland Security to augmenting an existing agency. Recommendations made since January 2002 are summarized next.

---

[150] Data from: *Securing the Homeland Strengthening the Nation,* 2002.

[151] *Making the Nation Safer,* Chap. 5. For details on activities until the beginning of January 2002, see CRS Report RL31202, pp. 37-38.

[152] *Making the Nation Safer,* p. ES-3.

[153] *Making the Nation Safer,* p. ES-9.

Appendix Table 2. Counterterrorism Programs Which Include Information Security R&D Funding (Dollars in millions)

	FY2002 Enacted (Base)	FY2002 Supp.	FY2003 Proposed
National Infrastructure Simulation and Analysis Center (Dept. of Energy)	$0	$0	$20
NSF: CIP Research and Physical and IT Security	198	0	197
Cybercorps R&D Training (NSF)	11	0	11
Computer Security Division, NIST	11	0	15

Source: *Securing the HomelandStrengthening the Nation,* 2002.

The CSIS focused on "threats emanating from the convergence of multiple technologies and sciences (e.g., information technology, nanotechnology, biotech, robotics, and microelectromechanical)." It said government has failed to provide among other things, "... the necessary investments in research and defensive and offensive tools to fulfill national security objectives." As a result, CSIS concluded: "A clear delegation of authority or chain of command both in the prevention and remediation of cyber attacks remains lacking. There also is no clear-cut authority for dealing with the issue of national information infrastructure protection."[154] According to William A. Wulf, president of the National Academy of Engineering, and Anita K. Jones, along with Wulf a professor of engineering at the University of Virginia, "... a particular government agency must take of the mission of revitalizing research in cyber-security with the following objectives:

> the development of wholly new methods of ensuring information system security, the development of a larger research community in cyber-security, and the education of computer system and computer science majors in cyber-security at the undergraduate level, which would eventually improve the state of the practice in industry."[155]

The third "Gilmore Report," concluded that "Enhanced R&D is critical to cyber-security. Technology is changing so rapidly that additional near-and long-term research is required. Many Federal agencies are engaged in

---

[154] Arnaud de Borchgrave, Frank J. Cilluffo, Sharon L. Cardash, Michèèle M. Ledgerwood, *Cyber Threats and Information Security Meeting the 21st Century Challenge,* CSIS, pp. 23-24.

[155] William A. Wulf and Anita K. Jones, "Cybersecurity," *The Bridge,* Spring 2002.

research development, test, and evaluation (RDT&E) in the cyber realm. However, no single comprehensive research agenda now exists that establishes priorities, prevents unnecessary duplication, and identifies gaps in current research." It recommended "... that the Office of Homeland Security develop and implement a comprehensive plan for RDT&E to enhance cyber-security. We envision a government-funded consortium of not-for-profit entities with expertise in the field. That entity can serve as the fulcrum for leveraging RDT&E resources in a manner consistent with national priorities for cyber-security."[156]

The National Academies observed that "no agency or department has the primary mission to foster progress" in information security.[157] It called for better coordination of R&D:

> DARPA and NSF created much of the science base for the Internet and for computer science in general, and other agencies — DOE, DOD, FBI, and NASA in particular — have made important contributions to computer-network technology. But the security of commercial computers is left largely to the private sector, and the present weakness in this area is a consequence of minimal market demand for it in the past. Coordination of agency efforts in this area is important, as is building a federal infrastructure to tap the intellectual and fiscal resources of private industry.[158]

Policy Actions since September 11, 2001

After the terrorist attacks, the Administration sought to develop a capability to coordinate cyber-security activities with the nation's counterterrorism effort and to better link information security R&D to these efforts. The mechanism developed has the potential to work effectively because it is closely linked to the antiterrorism effort and to the OSTP, and has specific authority to work with agencies to develop priority R&D programs and budgets.

---

[156] Advisory Panel to Assess Domestic Response Capabilities for Terrorism Involving Weapons of Mass Destruction, *Third Annual Report to the President and the Congress, III. For Ray Downey,* Dec. 15, 2001, p. 45.

[157] *Making the Nation Safer,* p. 12-17.

[158] *Making the Nation Safer,* p. 12-17.

In Executive Order 13231, October 16, 2001,[159] President Bush created "The President's Critical Infrastructure Protection Board," charged with preventing disruptions of critical infrastructure and information networks in water, telecommunication, financial, transportation, health care, emergency services and manufacturing. Although it is directed to work closely with industry and State and local governments, it is composed wholly of executive agency officials, including the OSTP Director and 24 other agency heads and officials. It is chaired by the Special Advisor to the President for Cyber Space Security, who reports both to the Assistant for National Security and the Assistant for Homeland Security. On October 9, 2001, President Bush named Richard Clarke, the Clinton Administration Critical Infrastructure coordinator, to serve as his special advisor on Cyber Space Security and director of the President's Critical Infrastructure Protection Board.[160] He was not specifically mentioned on the organizational chart as a member of the senior-level OHS Principals Committee, but he was listed among those who will attend meetings of the sub-Cabinet Deputies Committee if cyber-security is discussed.[161]

The Board, which was given responsibility "to recommend policies and coordinate programs," was charged to

> Coordinate with the Director of the Office of Science and Technology Policy (OSTP) on a program of Federal Government research and development for protection of information systems for critical infrastructure, including emergency preparedness communications, and the physical assets that support such systems, and ensure coordination of government activities in this field with corporations, universities, federally funded research centers, and national laboratories.

The executive order established 10 standing committees, including one on Research and Development, chaired by a designee of the Director of OSTP. In addition to proposing plans for "subjects within its purview," and making recommendations to OMB on agency budgets "that fall within the Board's purview, after review of relevant program requirements and resources," the Board was given specific authority to "annually request the

---

159 Executive Order 13231, "Critical Infrastructure Protection in the Information Age," Oct. 16, 2001, 66 FR 53063 to 66 FR53071.

160 "Fact Sheet on New Counter-Terrorism and Cyberspace Positions," White House Press Secretary, Oct. 9, 2001; "White House Bush Establishes New Positions For Fighting Terrorism, Cyberspace Security," *Daily Report for Executives*, Oct. 10, 2001, p. A-44.

161 Bar Vaida, "Cybersecurity Adviser Gets Second-tier Role in Homeland Defense," *GovExec.com*, Oct. 31, 2001.

National Science Foundation, Department of Energy, Department of Transportation, Environmental Protection Agency, Department of Commerce, Departments of Defense, and the Intelligence Community … to include in their budget requests to OMB funding for demonstration projects and research to support the Board's activities."

Since last fall, Clarke appears to have been actively guiding information security R&D activities, and has been quoted several times as having remarked that the private sector is not supporting sufficient amounts of cyber-security R&D or paying enough attention to correcting vulnerabilities in information systems.[162] The Administration apparently is seeking to expand partnerships with the private sector and encourage information sharing among industrial firms to help prevent attacks on computer systems. Reportedly, it "is formulating a tool called the *Cyber Warning and Information Network to* warn public and private sector businesses of impending cyber attacks, such as computer viruses that can hijack critical systems."[163] The Administration also seeks to develop an large Cybercorps program, which allocates scholarships totaling about $30,000 annually to students who choose to study information technology security issues[164] and urged universities to cooperate in developing a framework for cyber-security R&D.[165] The NSTC working group on "Protection of Vulnerable Systems" may engage in R&D priority-setting and coordination for information security R&D.

CONGRESSIONAL OPTIONS

There are no provisions in H.R. 5005 relating to information security R&D. S. 2452 would transfer the NIST computer security division, which conducts R&D, to the Critical Infrastructure Protection Division (sec. 133) and would give the Under Secretary for Critical Infrastructure Protection

---

[162] See, "Cybersecurity Czar Issues Wake-up Call to Industry, Agencies," *GovExec.Com,* Feb. 20, 2002; Anandashankar Mazumdar, "Computer Security, Administration Point Man on Cybersecurity Says Private Sector Aid Essential to Security," *Daily Report for Executives,* Dec. 5, 2001, p. A-15; and Maureen Shirhal, "While House Official Outlines Cybersecurity Initiatives," *GovExec.Com,* Jan. 25, 2002.

[163] Sirhal, Jan. 25, 2002.

[164] Sirhal, Jan. 25, 2002. See also: William New, "Cybersecurity Chief Assesses Progress," *GovExec.Com,* Feb. 13, 2002.

[165] Dan Carnevale, "White House Official Asks Colleges to Help Create National Counter-Security Strategy," *Chronicle of Higher Education,* Apr. 10, 2002.

some responsibilities for cyber-security. The extent of the proposed Under Secretary's responsibility for information security R&D priority setting and leadership of cooperative activities was not detailed.

The following are other major active bills that relate to counter-terrorism R&D.

S. 1900, "Cyberterrorism Preparedness Act." Introduced January 28, 2002, it authorizes the National Institute of Standards and Technology to award $350 million over the next five years for development of cyber-security best practices, long-term cyber-security R&D, and related activities. No further action has occurred.

S. 1901, "Cyber-security Research and Education Act." Introduced January 28, 2002, it would fund new fellowships at the NSF and the National Security Agency, and would offer incentives for students and teachers to focus on cyber-security. The bill also directs the Comptroller General to study, collect data, and report on the cyber-security workforce and on academic cyber-security research facilities. It authorizes $35 million to carry out the provisions of the bill until 2005. No further action has occurred.

H.R. 3394, "Cyber-security Research and Development Act"/S. 2182. Passed in the House on February 7,2002, it authorizes $875 million over the next five years for research and other activities against cyber-terrorism. $568 million would go to NSF and the remainder to NIST for cyber-security R&D. New programs would include cyber-security research centers, undergraduate program grants, competitive fellowship grants, and joint university/industry programs to attract more researchers to the field of computer and network. A Senate companion bill, S. 2182, introduced on April 17, 2002 was ordered to be reported favorably, amended, on May 17, 2002.[166]

H.R. 3844, "Federal Information Security Management Act." Introduced on March 5, 2002, it would require the Director of NIST to establish an office to conduct research to determine the nature and extent of information security vulnerabilities and techniques for providing cost-effective information security. Hearings were held on May 2, 2002.

H.R. 1259, "Computer Security Enhancement Act of 2001." Passed in the House on November 27, 2001, it would among other things provide fellowships to students to study cyber-security, require a study by the National Academies on electronic authentication technologies, and require the Secretary of Commerce to promote increased use of security technologies for the nation's information infrastructure.

CONCLUDING OBSERVATIONS

As noted, coordination of information security R&D has been formalized within the office of the Special Advisor to the President for Cyber Space Security and the President's Critical Infrastructure Protection Board, which was also given some authority to require agencies to allocate budget resources to priority R&D topics that serve the board's agenda. See Table 8. The need to collaborate closely with industry in information security R&D and other aspects of infrastructure protection may have motivated creation of a separate interagency coordination mechanism for information security R&D. It remains to be determined how effectively this mechanism will be able to identify federal R&D priorities and compel agencies to allocate budgetary resources for projects to meet the board's requirements.

[166] Molly M. Peterson, "Cyber Security Research Boosted by Senate Panel," *National Journal News Service,* May 17, 2002.

Chapter 13

APPENDIX 4. NATIONAL ACADEMIES' ACTIVITIES

The National Academies created a 22-member Committee on the Science and Technology Agenda for Countering Terrorism. Funding for this work came from foundations and the Academies' own endowment, (reportedly it used $2 million of its endowment to start activities).[167] The resulting report, released in June 2002, identified seven "Urgent Research Opportunities," (see Appendix Table 3A) and organizational issues (see Appendix Table 3B), and recommended specific actions to enhance federal agency capabilities to fulfill counter terrorism S&T missions. For instance, it recommended that the Department of Agriculture "needs the capacity to perform and fund research on plant and animal diseases and to develop and deploy surveillance systems. An agricultural equivalent of the Centers for Disease Control and Prevention might be an appropriate approach." (See Chapters 3 and 4.)

---

[167] Wil Lepkowski, "Addition: Academies Detail War Plan," *Science and Policy Perspectives*, Jan. 3, 2002.

Appendix Table 3A. "Urgent Research Opportunities" Identified in National Academies' Report

1. Develop effective treatments and preventatives for known pathogens for which current responses are unavailable and for potential emerging pathogens.
2. Develop, test, and implement an intelligent, adaptive electric-power grid.
3. Advance the practical utility of data fusion and data mining for intelligence analysis, and enhance information security against cyberattacks.
4. Develop new and better technologies (e.g., protective gear, sensors, communications) for emergency responders.
5. Advance engineering design technologies and fire-rating standards for blast- and fire-resistant buildings.
6. Develop sensor and surveillance systems (for a wide range of targets) that create useful information for emergency officials and decision makers.
7. Develop new methods and standards for filtering air against both chemicals and pathogens as well as better methods and standards for decontamination.[168]

Appendix Table 3B. R&D and Organizational Issues in National Academies' Report

Nuclear and Radiological Threats
Human and Agricultural Health Systems
Toxic Chemicals and Explosive Materials
Information Technology
Energy Systems
Transportation Systems
Cities and Fixed Infrastructure
The Response of People to Terrorism
Complex and Interdependent Systems (systems engineering, threat modeling and infrastructure modeling)
The Significance of Crosscutting Challenges and Technologies (systems analyses and modeling; integrated data management; sensors and sensor networks; autonomous mobile robotic technologies; supervisory control and data acquisition (SCADA) systems; biometrics; and human and organizational factors)
Equipping the Federal Government to Counter Terrorism (coordination, analysis, OSTP, federal agencies)
Essential Partners in a National Strategy (cooperation with states, cities, universities)[169]

---

[168] *Making the Nation Safer,* op. cit., p. ES-3.
[169] *Making the Nation Safer,* op. cit., Chap. I.

The Academies made available on their website the text of 25 publications about science, policy and security,[170] briefed TSWG panels, initiated work on bioterrorism, largely within the IOM, and studied issues affecting universities arising out of terrorism events.[171] The National Academy of Engineering also initiated a "study of 'homeland defense' against terrorism," now in process.[172] Separate studies, some on contract for federal agencies, were initiated through the National Research Council and the IOM on such issues as the psychology and sociology of terrorists organizations agricultural bioterrorism, transportation security, water supply protection, chemistry and national security.[173]

[170] See [http://nap.edu/terror/index.html].

[171] Testimony of Richard Klausner, Feb. 5, 2002. A report of the meeting on "Balancing National Security and Open Scientific Communication: Implications of September 11th for the Research University," was posted at the Association of American Universities website at [http://AAU.edu/research/NARerport.html].

[172] Science Scope, *Science,* Sept. 21, 2001.

[173] These initiatives were inventoried at "Summary of Counter-Terrorism Initiatives by the National Academies," February 31, 2002, available on the AAU website in a list entitled NRC/IOM Reports on Science and Technology for Countering Terrorism.

Chapter 14

APPENDIX 5. ACRONYMS

CBRN	Chemical, Biological, Radiological, Nuclear
CBW	Chemical and Biological Warfare
CDC	Centers for Disease Control and Prevention
CSIS	Center for Strategic and International Studies
DARP	A Defense Advanced Research Projects Agency
DHS	Department of Homeland Security (Proposed)
DHHS	Department of Health and Human Services
DNHS	Department of National Homeland Security (Proposed)
DOD	Department of Defense
DOE	Department of Energy
DSB	Defense Science Board
E.O.	Executive Order
EOP	Executive Office of the President
FBI	Federal Bureau of Investigation
FDA	Food and Drug Administration
FEMA	Federal Emergency Management Agency
FOIA	Freedom of Information Act
GAO	General Accounting Office
HHS	Health and Human Service [Department]
HSC	Homeland Security Council
IBM	International Business Machines Corp.
IOM	Institute of Medicine
NAE	National Academy of Engineering
NAS	National Academy of Sciences
NIH	National Institute of Health
NRC	National Research Council

NSC	National Security Council
NSTC	National Science and Technology Council
OHS	Office of Homeland Security
OMB	Office of Management and Budget
OSTP	Office of Science and Technology Policy
PCAST	President's Council of Advisors on Science and Technology
PCC	Policy Coordination Committee
PWMD	Preparedness against Weapons of Mass Destruction Group
R&D	Research and Development
RDT&E	Research, Development, Test, and Evaluation
S&T	Science and Technology
TSWG	Technical Support Working Group
WMD	Weapons of Mass Destruction

INDEX

D

E

F

G

H